30 DAYS TO THE CO-TAUGHT CLASSROOM

30 DAYS

TO THE

Co-Taught Classroom

How to Create an
AMAZING,
Nearly
MIRACULOUS
& Frankly
EARTH-SHATTERING
Partnership in One Month or Less

DR. PAULA KLUTH & DR. JULIE CAUSTON

ISBN-13: 978-1546797425
ISBN-10: 1546797424
LCCN:

Distributed by

Cover Design by
Typeset by
Icon Graphics designed by Freepik
Illustrations by Ray Craighead
Book Design by Kevin Fitzgerald

Printed in the United States of America

CONTENTS

INTRODUCTION

Are you looking for help in your co-teaching journey, but finding you have little time to learn new strategies and skills? Well, you have come to the right place. We intend to teach you all you need to know about collaboration in 30 days. Yes, you read that right! In just 30 days, we will introduce you to the information, competencies and habits you will need to become a great co-teaching partner. We will help you get to know your co-teacher, understand your roles, improve your planning and co-planning skills, expand the structures you use to teach and support students and even celebrate your accomplishments.

Who We Are

We are both teachers and teacher educators who live and breathe inclusive education, differentiated instruction and collaboration. We have both been co-teachers in elementary, middle and high schools; professors in the area of inclusive education; and consultants to school districts, individual schools and families. Collectively, we have an abundance of lived experiences with co-teaching and have seen first-hand the amazing benefits (and, of course, the challenges) of this popular service delivery model.

Also, we both love long walks on the beach, sticky notes cut into fun little shapes (e.g., apples, arrows, letters of the alphabet) and books about animals who talk.

What's In The Book?

We have organized this book strategically. Every "day" of ideas builds on the information in previous "days" and is full of tips and suggestions you and your co-teacher can use immediately. Throughout the book, we provide a rationale for many of the practices associated with co-teaching to help you see the "why" as well as the "how" of the work. We have included dozens of tables and figures and short lists of "to do" reminders to help you remain focused on the most critical recommendations. Finally, we have peppered the pages with illustrations of our little team. These are provided to aid your comprehension and enjoyment of the material, but also to remind you that we are with you every step of the way in this process. Feel free to "clip and save" if you find these pics as irresistible as we do.

We begin this book with stuff that will get you started. That is, we jump right into meeting and getting to know your co-teacher, establishing your shared vision and goals and spreading the news about your co-teaching partnership.

Then, button up your shirt and straighten your tie. The next few sections are all business and are largely about planning. We discuss creating time to meet, running a meeting, honing collaborative habits of mind and so on.

After you have mastered the basics of teaming, we focus on teaching itself. We explore how to create a rockin' co-taught classroom. This includes designing an enviable classroom community, using a wide range of co-teaching structures and differentiating instruction until the cows come home.[1]

Finally, this book finishes with a smattering of ideas for "keeping it going." We don't want your co-teaching energy to fizzle after just 30 days. Therefore, we conclude with thoughts on solving problems, invigorating the co-taught classroom and gathering resources for further study.

---

1   Urban readers should understand this to mean "until the 7-Eleven closes."

Why 30 Days?

30 days is doable[2]. In roughly one month, you can communicate more effectively with your co-teacher, try new co-teaching formats, create a more collaborative classroom and learn how to share what you know with others.

We encourage you and your co-teacher to join thousands of other collaborative teams and take this 30-day challenge. To do so you each must:

1. *Commit to reading one section each day.*

2. *Meet for five to fifteen minutes after completing this reading assignment. Use this time to review the content and featured action items. In addition, be sure to discuss the jokes we share in these pages, as you may want to use them on your family and friends.*

3. *Act. Don't just read this book to impress people on the subway or in the coffee shop (though many likely will be wowed). Use it to bring your co-teaching dreams to fruition.*

How To Use The Book

This book is yours. Use it. Draw in the margins (unless it is from the library or you borrowed it from your co-teacher or you are thinking of drawing something really odd and unrelated to co-teaching in it). Read it again. Try out new concepts, even if you feel a bit out of your comfort zone when you do so. Complete every exercise. Have fun!

Though we wrote this book in a 30-day format to make it user-friendly, bite-sized and intriguing (did it work?), we realize this may not *literally* be a 30-day project for everyone. Take the challenge if you'd like and improve your co-teaching relationship and practices in roughly a month. Or feel free to pick and choose sections to read, skipping around and grabbing ideas here and there. Or, binge read it from cover to cover in a single day or weekend. It's up to you. We believe in offering options. That's just how we roll.

---

2   We did some research, and apparently, there are a lot of things one can accomplish in a month, including learn to play the ukulele, write a novel, build a gazebo and, for you fitness buffs out there, engage in something called the "Butts & Guts Challenge."

A Word About Our Favorite Word: *Inclusion*

Before we begin, we know you undoubtedly have a lot on your mind and are anxious to dive into conversations about collaboration, planning your shared space and coordinating outfits on the first day of school, but we, as your mentors-on-paper, feel it is our duty to slow you down a bit and help you remember that the reason you are even reading this book is to better serve all students. Together. That means everyone. In an inclusive classroom. With teachers who embrace inclusive education. Did we mention involving everyone? Inclusively? As in "all means all"?

So, let's start your work as co-teachers reviewing what inclusion is and how it fits into a co-teaching framework.

What Inclusion Is

A common understanding of inclusive education is that it is a model of service delivery where students with and without disabilities are educated in age-appropriate, general education classes in their neighborhood schools. This definition is a good start, but we feel inclusive schooling is much more than a way to support students with identified needs.

Inclusion, to us, is not only about disability. It is about every learner in the classroom being valued and seen as an important member of the school, including students from all racial and ethnic groups, students new to the school, English language learners and students with diverse family constellations. Inclusion, therefore, means making sure that every learner feels socially connected and welcome in the classroom and in the school. It means honoring the social needs of students as well as their academic needs and treating all members of the school community with dignity and respect.

In addition, we feel inclusion is not simply about our practices as educators but our approach to our work. This ideology is certainly about designing responsive curriculum and instruction, but it is also about considering issues of equity. Inclusion means exploring structures, practices and norms that create barriers for any student.

Finally, we see inclusion as a strategy for transforming schools and supporting teachers. We see it as a belief system in which educators value what each and every student brings to the classroom. It is about empowering and supporting the whole individual for the good of the entire community. As Shapiro-Barnard (1998) illustrates, inclusion can be seen as a reform that can help all students find belonging and success in schools:

Even if there were not students with disabilities, the culturing of inclusive schools would still be important because the entrance of students with disabilities into general education classes does not signify the presence of diversity in the school; it recognizes and affirms the diversity that has always existed. As a result, people are less bound by false ideals of normalcy, are less fearful of expressing their own uniqueness, and thus are more able to learn. (p. 12)

Co-Teaching & Inclusion

While there are exceptions to the rule, most co-teaching relationships start because of a school's or district's desire to better support diverse learners and to grow an inclusive schooling model. One can happen without the other, and we have definitely seen great inclusive schools without co-teaching models and effective co-teaching models in schools that lack a commitment to equity and inclusion.

We believe, however, that combining a great collaboration model with high-quality inclusive schooling practices is the best of all worlds, the bee's knees, the cat's meow, the gold standard and da bomb dot com. So, we are crossing our fingers and hoping that you are starting this work by committing not only to learning more about collaboration but also to using your new role as a co-teacher to include, support and welcome diverse learners in ways you could only dream about when you were on your own without a partner at your side. So, if you have been reticent in the past, go ahead and take this opportunity to embrace inclusive education with wild abandon. While you are at it, embrace your co-teaching partner too. It can't hurt, and it just might help you get past that awkward, "I wonder if this person is a hugger and will ever randomly embrace me?" phase. Feel better? We thought so.

At this point, we recommend that you sit close together and place your hands on the top right corner of this page. Yes, you read that right. You are going to be planning together, teaching together and working as a team. Do you really think we want you to turn the first page of the 30-day challenge all on your own? Not a chance. So pinch those fingers, grasp this fine-quality paper, lift and turn as a team and complete your first act of collaboration and cooperation. Go ahead. We will be waiting on the next page for both of you.

DAY 1

MEET & GREET

It may not be as nerve-racking as a middle school first date, but meeting the person you will teach with side-by-side, day in and day out, can be a bit of a nail-biter. This is especially true for educators who have limited experience with collaborative planning or teaching.

In some instances, co-teaching partnerships are formed from educators making recommendations and providing input. In other cases, however, teams will be assembled by administrators, and teachers may find out about their pairings blind-date style. That is, they may be thrown together with little knowledge about their respective partners and sometimes with little time to get acquainted. In these situations, it is best to do as much "getting to know you" work in as little time as possible. Hopefully, this will mean an informal initial meeting followed by some more structured opportunities to learn about and from one another.

Initial Meeting

The first job of co-teaching partners is to simply get to know one another on a personal level. Do this before diving into conversations about room setup, materials storage, lesson plan formats and preferred fonts for the interactive whiteboard.

In some schools, structured activities are offered to help co-teachers become acquainted. We think these types of teambuilding activities are key to starting relationships off on the right foot. You might play a whole-staff game of mini-golf with your co-teacher as your partner or watch a fun buddy-style flick with other co-teaching teams. Trust us, when you become irritated about the coffee rings your co-teacher leaves on your desk, or his never-ending knock-knock jokes, it will be helpful to have the sweet memory of that spinning-merry-go-round, into-the-creepy-clown-nose, hole-in-one victory, or your shared fondness for *Harold & Kumar Go to White Castle.*

If your school or district does not offer an opportunity to formally connect before teaching begins, consider kicking off the year with some type of informal off-campus socializing. This might be something as simple as having lunch at a neighborhood restaurant, attending a talk or reading together or even doing some shopping for the classroom (see Figure 1.1 for additional teambuilding ideas). The activity you choose *isn't* important, but making time to connect before the school year begins *is*.

If you can't find time for any socializing before the bell rings on day one, at least schedule a lunch or two during that first week of school to ensure that you have some common ground to work from when students enter the classroom. This time can be used to talk about your past teaching experiences and to share some of your views and values as educators. We think it is also helpful to share personal likes, dislikes and interests at this time—after all, you are not just coworkers, you are becoming roommates (at least for some period of time during the day).

Q & A

We know that this getting-to-know-you routine can seem odd to some—especially to those who already have a professional relationship with their new partner, so we recommend structuring this conversation a bit with our handy dandy "20 Questions for Co-Teachers" Activity (see Figure 1.2). Some of these questions are light and humorous, but others are more serious and are more directly connected to classroom work. Prompts like, "I wish I was better at _____" can help you learn about the supports you might provide for your partner. So if one of you says, "I wish I was better at organizing," the other may be able to chime in with encouragement, ideas or offers to help. Questions like, "What is your favorite tech tool in the classroom?" may help you to learn about resources while getting a feel for your partner's comfort level when it comes to trying new things. So, while some teachers may find these exercises tedious or silly, we find them to be critical in setting the stage for success. Further, the question about coolest/weirdest toy will give you a rare opportunity to brag about your circa 1978 Stretch Armstrong doll. You are welcome.

IMPLEMENTATION TIP

If you don't have time to go through the "20 Questions" game today, tuck this list into your plan book and revisit one question in each of your team meetings this year. This can be a lighthearted launch into your planning and a way to keep connecting with your partner all year long.

Teambuilding Now & Later

So, you should be off to the races with your co-teaching partner by now—literally. Okay, so it doesn't have to be the races, but you should have selected some activity or some time to get to know one another. If you did that, we congratulate you. We are thrilled and we hope it went well, but we want to let you know that while your first meeting will be a great opportunity for connecting on a personal level, it should not be the only time you engage in this type of interaction. Of course, these types of exercises may happen more regularly in the beginning of the year, but teambuilding should never really end if you want to have a healthy classroom partnership.

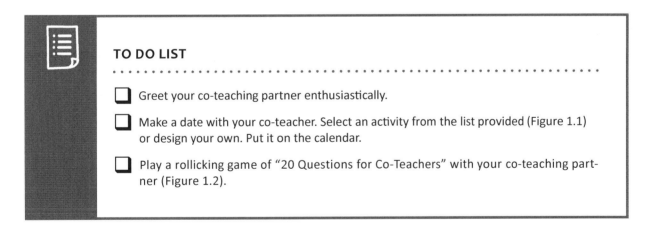

TO DO LIST

☐ Greet your co-teaching partner enthusiastically.

☐ Make a date with your co-teacher. Select an activity from the list provided (Figure 1.1) or design your own. Put it on the calendar.

☐ Play a rollicking game of "20 Questions for Co-Teachers" with your co-teaching partner (Figure 1.2).

FIGURE 1.1
Teambuilding Activity Checklist

Choose at least one activity for a one-time outing, one activity you would like to engage in at least twice a year and one activity for weekly or monthly teambuilding. Start by highlighting any activity that you think would be potentially useful or fun. Next, put a (#) by your idea for a one-time outing, a (✓) by anything you might try twice this year and a (!) by something you might want to use on a regular basis.

_____ coffee klatch

_____ potluck lunch

_____ walk and talk/
run and talk

_____ before-school breakfast

_____ off-site professional
development seminar

_____ collaborative webinar
tune-in

_____ collaborative tweeting/
Facebook posting/blogging

_____ off-site lecture

_____ book club
(personal or professional)

_____ after-school
board game
tournament

_____ geocaching

_____ department or
grade-level charades

_____ sing along/karaoke

_____ paint ball

_____ intramural sports

_____ bowling

_____ hiking

_____ dance chaperoning

_____ laser tag

_____ fieldtrip site scouting

_____ classroom decorating
or arranging

_____ crafting/scrapbooking

_____ co-volunteering for
charity (e.g., school blood
drive)

_____ buddy-themed movie night
(e.g., *Thelma & Louise*,
Turner & Hooch)

_____ concerts in the park

_____ Pinterest pin party

_____ knitting circle

_____ bake-off/cook-off

List other potential teambuilding activities here:

> _____

> _____

> _____

> _____

> _____

> _____

> _____

> _____

> _____

> _____

> _____

> _____

FIGURE 1.2
20 Questions for Co-Teachers

Use this list of questions as a way to get to know your co-teacher. Revisit these questions and others like them throughout the year to become personally and professionally acquainted with your partner.

1. *What do you think will be the best thing about our co-taught classroom?*

2. *Why did you become a teacher?*

3. *What is the last book you read?*
   What is the last magazine you read?
   What is the last cereal box side panel you read?

4. *Do you like candy corn? Why or why not?*

5. *What is your favorite lesson of the year?*

6. *What is one school supply you cannot live without?*

7. *What is your worst habit?*

8. *What is your favorite movie? What is your favorite movie about co-teaching?*

9. *What is the worst hairstyle/haircut you ever had?*

10. *What is your best joke?*

11. *What is the coolest/weirdest toy you had as a child?*

12. *What do you like about the first day of school?*

13. *What is your favorite classroom tech tool (e.g., website, app, piece of assistive tech)?*

14. *Fill in the blank: "I wish I was better at _____."*

15. *Fill in the blank: "I am one of the best _____ I know."*

16. *Fill in the blank: "I like a classroom to feel like a _____."*

17. *In one word, what is your philosophy of education?*

18. *What was your prom song? What should it have been?*

19. *If you wrote a book for other teachers, what would the title be?*

20. *Are you thrilled, excited, over-the-moon or only a bit delighted to have me as your co-teaching partner?*

HAVE A VISION

You can start to build a remarkable co-teaching partnership right away by exploring a few simple questions as a team: What do we want to do? What do we expect? What is our dream? In other words, you should begin your collaboration by determining where you want to go together.

Why Do We Need A Vision?

Teaching teams should share some core values about learners, teaching and the school community if they are to have success reaching all students. For this reason, you and your partner should craft a vision statement that will clearly communicate shared intentions and serve as a tool for making decisions and guiding daily classroom practices.

To some, visioning work seems unnecessary. It may even be seen as a waste of precious time, but we believe that teams who are willing to take a few minutes to create a vision and use it as a guide-post for planning will quickly understand its power. We believe strongly in using a classroom vision as a tool for collaboration, communication and transformation. In fact, we see a shared articulated vision as a potential game changer for both teachers and their students.

Visioning can:

» *create a shared sense of purpose*
» *help co-teaching teams crystalize ideas, beliefs and goals*
» *help co-teaching teams create priorities*
» *provide a specific focus for daily, monthly and long-term planning*
» *guide daily work*
» *guide daily decisions*
» *inspire big thinking*

So, a middle school team that has a vision of high achievement for all learners, eliminating pull-out supports during their shared social studies and language arts classes and getting all students to become more enthusiastic readers, will have a clear focus as they plan necessary supports (e.g., peer tutoring); consider the conversations they need to have with administrators, families, students and therapists (e.g., brainstorm ideas for "push in" services); decide on classroom practices (e.g., active learning); and find or develop new materials (e.g., a wider variety of books in multiple formats).

When teams have a vision in place, daily decisions can be based on big picture goals and ideas and can be assessed based on values and priorities. Without a vision, day-to-day and lesson-to-lesson planning can lack both clarity and inspiration.

What Do We Include?

So, now that you are sold on the idea of visioning, get ready to brainstorm. As you sit down to do this work, ask, "What do we want for ourselves, our students and our classroom?" Other questions that can guide this work include:

> » *What is the purpose of teaching?*
> » *How do students learn best?*
> » *What does the ideal classroom/lesson/learning community look and feel like?*
> » *In what kind of a classroom would we like to learn?*
> » *In what kind of classroom do we want to teach?*
> » *What do we want students to remember about our co-taught classroom?*

As you begin to draft some statements, draw pictures or jot down ideas, be sure to:

> » *draw on the existing mission of your school or district;*
> » *be audacious, grand and daring;*
> » *be specific;*
> » *be open to interrogating old practices; and*
> » *be open to reimagining "what can be."*

As you work on your vision, be aware of behaviors that can sabotage your efforts. These behaviors include but are not limited to:

> » *creating a vision just because you read about it in this book, to "get it over with" or to please your administrator or co-teaching partner;*
> » *focusing on what you want to avoid versus focusing on what you want to have or achieve;*
> » *failing to dream beyond your current circumstances;*
> » *seeing current structures, norms and policies as intractable; and*
> » *trying to nail down a plan before or at the same time as you are crafting your vision.*

Create

Imagine. It is the end of the school year and you have created the most remarkable classroom, supported students to succeed beyond your wildest expectations and developed a stunningly effective co-teaching partnership. With your co-teaching partner, envision, describe, draw, sculpt, dance or otherwise illustrate this vision. You can use the workspace provided in Figure 2.1, lay out your ideas on chart paper or create your vision using a tech tool such as PowerPoint or Prezi (www.prezi.com). Try to answer at least the following questions in your vision statement, presentation or poster:

» *What does the classroom environment look like (e.g., seating, walls, teaching materials, technology)?*
» *What are the teachers doing?*
» *What are members of the support staff doing (e.g., therapists, paraprofessionals)?*
» *What are the students doing?*
» *What can you hear in the classroom?*
» *How do the students feel?*
» *How do the educators feel?*
» *What are others saying/thinking/observing about your classroom?*

When you are done, sit back and admire this work of art. If you have taken our advice to dream big, to get specific, to include details and to keep your vision clear and accessible to you both, you will have a powerful road map that can be used to inspire a year of success.

TO DO LIST
. . . .

☐ Discuss the ideal co-taught classroom with your co-teaching partner.

☐ Create a vision statement/drawing/collage/sculpture/interpretive dance as a team.

☐ Collectively admire the vision statement/drawing/collage/sculpture/interpretive dance you have created.

FIGURE 2.1

Classroom Vision Workspace

Create an image of your ideal classroom. Use words, phrases, pictures and anything else you feel will help you and your co-teaching partner create the best possible environment, culture and circumstances for student learning and growth.

DAY 3

SET GOALS

Now that you have a vision for your work, your students and your classroom, we will turn our attention to setting specific goals. Of course, some goals are already set for us as educators. We are expected to support students in meeting certain benchmarks, in succeeding on formal and informal assessments and in reaching their individualized education program (IEP) goals. The goals we are targeting on Day 3, however, are not dictated by administrators, the state or school boards; we are going to explore the goals that you personally want to set for your teaching and for your co-teaching partnership.

Explore Targets For Teaching & Teachers

Goals are critical to the health of a co-teaching partnership. Like your vision, your goals provide a focus. They also offer a way to assess the efficacy of your teaching and your teaming.

You will want to use your co-constructed vision [Day 2] as a jumping-off point for developing goals; think about what you hope to achieve and how you can achieve it. For example, if you have a vision of creating the most welcoming classroom imaginable, you might want to set goals related to acquiring classroom materials, designing learning spaces, communicating with families or meeting student sensory needs.

The following goals can be used as conversation starters or even adopted "as is" by you and your co-teaching partner:

Goals for Teaching

» *We will raise our standardized test scores by 10% this year.*
» *We will graduate every eighth grade student.*
» *We will hold a twenty-minute writing conference with every student every month.*
» *We will use at least eighteen different collaborative exercises in our classroom this year.*
» *We will attend a seminar on autism to better support our students on the spectrum.*
» *We will call every parent at least twice during the school year to share good news.*

Goals for Co-Teachers

» *We will use at least four different co-teaching structures each week of this semester.*
» *We will start and end our co-planning meetings on time.*
» *We will design co-taught lessons with our speech pathologist, occupational therapist and social worker at least twice during each quarter of the school year.*
» *We will co-teach and co-plan with every one of our thirty students this year.*
» *We will each read three co-selected books on co-teaching this year, meeting after we finish each one to discuss our favorite ideas.*
» *We will dress in matching content-related outfits three times this year.*
» *We will engage in one long-range planning session four times per year (August 30, October 1, January 15 and March 5).*

Notice that these goals are all observable and measurable. That is, anyone evaluating progress on them would be able to tell what to assess. A goal of "increasing the use of augmentative communication opportunities in daily instruction" is not sufficient because it is unclear what types of supports or strategies are being targeted, what student or teacher behaviors should change or be encouraged and what exact marker or indicator would constitute success. A goal of "providing at least three opportunities for all students to use augmentative or alternative communication each day (e.g., sign language, dry erase paddles)", however, is both specific and easy to evaluate.

Write Your Own

Now, go ahead and set some of your own goals using the worksheet in Figure 3.1. When you finish, keep this page handy so you can remember your priorities and assess your progress throughout the year.

IMPLEMENTATION TIP

Determine where you will keep your vision statement and goals. Consider laminating and posting them, placing them in a binder with your team notes, making a Glogster poster (edu.glogster. com) or uploading materials to a shared Dropbox (www.dropbox.com) folder. Choose any space that allows you to review and update these items regularly.

TO DO LIST

☐ Take a good look at your co-teaching vision. Using it as a planning tool, set at least three goals for the classroom and three goals for your co-teaching relationship.

☐ Check your goals to make sure they are observable. Now make sure they are measurable. Now make sure they are fabulous.

☐ Put it out there. Tell someone else (e.g., your administrator, another colleague, the copy machine repair person) about the daring goals you have set.

FIGURE 3.1
Co-Teaching Goal-Setting Form

OUR GOALS!

Record three goals for your work with students. Goals can cover anything from what you want students to achieve to what you want to try instructionally. For example: "We will raise our standardized test scores by 10% this year."

☐ #1 _____

_____

☐ #2 _____

_____

☐ #3 _____

_____

Now, write three goals specifically for your co-teaching relationship or co-teaching practices. For example: "We will use at least four different co-teaching structures each week of this semester."

☐ #1 _____

_____

☐ #2 _____

_____

☐ #3 _____

_____

DAY 4

SHARE THE NEWS

So, you are ready to support your inclusive classroom... right? You have learned a bit about your co-teaching partner... yes? You have set some audacious goals...correct? Well, that is a lot of work. Congratulations!

We are impressed, but we don't think we are the only ones who will be awestruck by your commitment and accomplishments. It's clearly time to brag a bit and let others know what you are up to. Let's focus on the audiences who will be most invested in the changes you have in mind for the classroom this year—your colleagues, parents and students.

Sharing With Colleagues

Depending on where you teach and the norms of your building, you may have very little you need to share. In some places, nearly every teacher in the building is collaborating and co-teaching so practices related to this work are commonplace and need little explanation. In other schools, however, you and your partner may be the only teachers taking on new roles, and your colleagues may need a bit of education on how you will be functioning in the classroom and how it might impact them. For instance, you may want to let other teachers know how to communicate with you and your partner (e.g., Do all communications go to both of you or are some matters of business handled by just one of you?); clarify any new language you are using (e.g., Do you need to remind colleagues that you are both teachers and that you and your partner are not highlighting identities like "special education teacher" and "general education teacher"?); and explain how you will distribute roles and responsibilities so that when they see you in a one teach/one observe model, they don't mistakenly think that the teacher who is not delivering the lesson (but is taking observational notes on a clipboard) is available for a quick discussion.

Sharing With Parents

Families may also need a bit of help to understand the function, purposes and norms of a co-teaching team. Parents may want to know, for instance, why their child is in a co-taught classroom, what the classroom will look/feel/sound like with two teachers instead of one and how (and if) they should communicate with two educators (Murawski, 2009). You can certainly attempt to answer parent questions as they arise or you can construct and send an email describing your work and the rationale for it like these two savvy middle school teachers did:

Dear Families:

We are writing to introduce ourselves and share a few details about your child's co-taught earth science class.

Co-teaching has recently been adopted by several schools in our district due to its many benefits. In co-taught classrooms, teachers get to collaborate in lesson design and capitalize on the experiences of two professionals with different areas of expertise. In addition, this model will allow us to teach using a much wider variety of lesson formats. For example, we will regularly be able to work with students in small groups or even split the class in half to bring our teacher-student ratio down from 2:32 to 1:16.

As the year goes on, please do not hesitate to contact us with any questions you have about our co-teaching model or related practices. In addition, please talk to your eighth graders about their impressions of their co-taught classroom. We intend to make students our partners in this endeavor and plan to involve them in our collaboration so that they can help us support their learning differences, create engaging daily lessons and make science more interesting and comprehensible for all.

We can be reached through our website, via e-mail or by calling the school between 3:00-4:00 p.m. You are always welcome to speak with either one of us about your child and his or her needs. Be assured that concerns or ideas shared with one teacher will always be shared with the other.

We look forward to a successful and collaborative school year!

Sincerely,

Ms. Dee Crane & Ms. Elinor LaPlant

In addition to a welcome letter, consider conducting a collaborative back-to-school night or open house presentation. This way, parents can learn about your partnership as they observe it in action.

To keep families informed as the year goes on, create tools to communicate your commitment to collaboration. One team we know occasionally blogs about their partnership (see Figure 4.1). Another creates short videos about their practices and posts them on their class website. Still another hosts before-school coffees to share details of their work with interested families.

FIGURE 4.1
Co-Teaching Blog Post

Sharing With Students

Now we will address the most important stakeholders—your students. We are constantly amazed when teachers tell us that they have talked to everyone about their co-teaching relationship except their students. Students are your partners in this journey. They are part of your collaborative team and need to be informed about your co-teaching aims and practices as much as—if not more than—any other group. There are probably dozens of ways to share your work with students, but because we have a lot to cover in this resource-rich text, we are going to share only two: showing and telling, and connecting to your curriculum.

Show & Tell

In a blog post on *MiddleWeb*, the popular website designed for middle-grade teachers, teacher Elizabeth Stein relays a story that illustrates how important it is to explicitly communicate the goals, intentions and practices of co-teaching to learners. Stein shares that she and her co-teaching partner were having a conversation with the class about their collaboration, and they decided to ask students some questions about their practice. First, they posed questions about the benefits of a co-teaching model. Students were positive in their responses and shared that they appreciated the extra help available in co-taught classrooms. They also noted that it was nice to have consistency when one teacher was sick and that they liked having another teacher to clarify points and lead discussions.

When asked, however, about the "why" of co-teaching, students gave answers that were both illuminating and disappointing for their teachers. Most of the students said that two teachers were needed for "special education" students or for those with learning problems. When asked a verbal follow-up question of, "Are both teachers here to help all students?" the entire class answered with a resounding "Noooooo!" (www.middleweb.com/5729/what-kids-say-about-inclusion/).

These teachers had worked hard to demonstrate parity, equality and role sharing and to communicate that both teachers were there for all students, but they quickly realized that they still had work to do to create their ideal collaborative classroom. Stein and her co-teaching partner immediately started assessing their practice to see how they could convey the rationale of their work with its beneficiaries.

Stein's story highlights the importance of educating students about co-teaching on the first day of school and keeping that conversation going all year long. This is not a talk you want to have just once; it is a discussion you would want to have repeatedly as the need arises or as the subject comes up. For instance, if a student with a disability asks for "his teacher" when he is stumped on a question, he can be reminded that he has two teachers in the classroom. Or when students are working in a parallel structure, let them know why you have chosen this structure (e.g., to offer students choices; to temporarily shrink the class size). This will help your students see how co-teaching benefits them. Further, students—especially those in middle and high school—can become savvier consumers of co-teaching when they are informed and can, therefore, offer critiques and suggestions of daily lessons that may be useful to your team and to other students.

Connect To Curriculum

Co-teaching can also be taught explicitly as part of the curriculum. It doesn't have to be an entire unit or featured on your curriculum-based assessments, but there are plenty of ways to integrate co-teaching information into the daily work of the classroom and even into standards-based lessons.

You can bring co-teaching into daily examples and illustrations. For instance, you might introduce collaboration when you teach analogies (e.g., "Co-teaching is like a marriage because…") or when you are teaching about alliteration (e.g., "Co-teachers cover content but also are awesome at allowing all to achieve academically") or even when you are learning about historical figures (e.g., "Marie and Pierre Curie were equal partners in their quest to discover chemical elements, just like your two teachers are equal partners in this quest for imparting skills and knowledge to sixth-grade science students").

Common teaching strategies can also be used creatively to make your points. You might have older students engage in a close reading of an article on co-teaching. This invitation to "step behind the teacher's desk" and learn about the work of the educator is often welcomed by learners and can inspire a rich classroom conversation. Or you could make an anchor chart exploring what students know about collaboration and co-teaching. Or work with students to create a Venn diagram (see Figure 4.2) comparing and contrasting the two teachers on your team.

We know there are plenty of other ways to teach these ideas of collaboration, connection and co-teaching, so take some time to brainstorm your own curriculum links. Students will likely get a kick out of your efforts, and you and your partner may find that having a new lens, example or visual related to your work is motivating for the teachers in the classroom too.

FIGURE 4.2
Venn Diagram Comparing Teachers in a Co-Taught Classroom

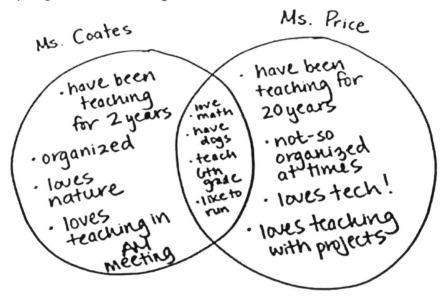

TO DO LIST

☐ Create a message to send to colleagues about your co-teaching partnership. Send it.

☐ Design a product (e.g., letter, postcard, blog post) to teach families about your co-teaching relationship. Share it.

☐ Choose at least one way to teach a bit about co-teaching. Put it into a lesson.

DAY 5

TAKE TIME TO MAKE TIME

Finding time to collaborate is one of the biggest challenges for co-teachers. We work with co-teaching teams across the country, and we repeatedly hear that there is not enough time to meet and to discuss students, lessons, assessments and so on. This issue is of particular concern for special education teachers who may be working with more than one general education teacher or for general education teachers collaborating closely with more than one specialist. We also hear complaints from teaching teams that are frustrated by the lack of options for meeting with paraprofessionals and other support staff. Quite simply, there seems to be a lot of need for meeting time and not enough minutes to go around.

So, what is a committed but time-strapped team to do? We recommend engaging in a quick assess-ment of needs and then working together to negotiate, borrow or steal the time you need. There is no other option. Finding time, making that time sacred and using that time efficiently is critical to your collaborative success.

Assessing Needs

Ask yourselves the following questions:

> » *What do we need to discuss face-to-face?*
> » *What might we be able to handle via text, e-mail, on-line planning tools or through any other method of communication?*
> » *How much time are we already given to meet? Is that up for negotiation? If you said, "No" are you sure? Are you totally sure? One hundred percent sure? Check again. We'll wait. Oh... you are pretty sure then?*
> » *Do we need more time?*
> » *How can we carve out more time if we need it?*
> » *Who can we ask about getting more time if we need it?*
> » *How can we help our administrators help us? In other words, do we have some specific ideas for getting more time if it is needed?*

Depending on your answers to these questions, you will potentially want to talk to other teaching teams and administrators about next steps. In some cases, you will answer these questions and realize you have all of the time you need. In other cases, you may learn that you need ideas for creating more time together. If so, read on.

Finding Time At The Table

If you are co-teaching for all or most of your day, you need to carve out some formal planning time with your co-teaching partner. We recommend a minimum of sixty minutes each week, plus a couple of additional fifteen-minute meetings to iron out any changes or challenges that arise from day to day. In addition, we suggest adding one multi-hour meeting to your schedule every few months (e.g., 3:00-5:00 p.m.) to draft several weeks of plans, discuss progress of students and plan for any changes to instructional practices.

So, now that you know what's needed, prepare to secure your meeting time. In most instances, this is a job for school leaders. If your administrators are looking for ideas, share these three suggestions for creating face-to-face meeting time: plan for planning, plan to pay and eliminate duties.

Plan For Planning

Ideally, co-teachers will have time built into their schedules for planning. For middle school and high school teachers this likely means designating at least one planning period a week for a co-teaching meeting. For elementary teachers, this means using or creating student-free times during the week. In some schools, leaders designate a planning day each week. On these days, the related services staff keep their schedules free for the meetings and a team of substitute teachers rotates around the school to cover the classrooms of the various educators scheduled for planning.

Plan To Pay

If finding plan time or substitute teachers is a challenge in your district, paying for planning is an option you may want to consider. In this model, teams choose when they will meet (e.g., Thursdays from 3:30–5:00 p.m.) and receive compensation for the time they spend at the planning table.

IMPLEMENTATION TIP

. . . .

Are you planning to ask your administration for some paid planning time? Write a short proposal. Include the purpose of meeting(s), staff required, targeted goals and how you will report outcomes to the administration.

Eliminate Duties

Lunch aides, playground staff or study hall monitors can be hired so teachers are free to plan during times when they would typically be engaged in student supervision. Hiring extra support staff is typically less expensive than hiring substitute teachers, so this is often an attractive option for financially-strapped districts.

Moving To Plan B

Do you think the ideas so far are just wishful thinking? Are you still skeptical about getting enough planning time built into your schedule? If so, it may be time for Plan B. There are alternatives to structured planning time that other teams have used successfully. Discuss the following ideas with your collaborative partner and decide if any of them can work for you.

Ask For Independence

Create a weekly meeting time where students are expected to watch a video, work on technology-driven tasks like virtual fieldtrips or WebQuests, engage in peer tutoring lessons or otherwise work independently for fifteen to thirty minutes. If possible, have a classroom paraprofessional facilitate the learning experience.

Show Up Before Or Stay After

Utilize thirty minutes before or after school starts once or twice each week.

Do Lunch

And make it satisfying! Have this be a day where you order out or picnic in the classroom and share the contents of your lunch boxes. These lunch dates may not be filled with fun every week, but they should be as pleasant as possible and—here is the tough part—as structured as your other meetings. One drawback to lunch meetings is that you may get into the spirit of eating, talking and sharing and totally forget to stay on track with an agenda. Or you might make the mistake of forgoing meeting notes so you can use two hands to devour the leftover ribs you brought. Consider yourselves warned. If you select this option, we suggest that you always keep in mind that lunch meetings are still meetings. To keep on track, we suggest that you consider meeting outside the lounge and that you remember to take notes and follow meeting guidelines as you would elsewhere.

Volunteer A Volunteer

While a parent or community volunteer reads a book, leads a review game or teaches art lessons, meet together for a few minutes in the back of the room. Don't have volunteers? Consider advertising for one or more to amp up your goals and create new learning opportunities for your team and your students.

Travel With The Team

Put two classrooms (preferably co-taught classrooms) together for thirty to sixty minutes each week for a certain portion of the curriculum, community-building exercises or group activities such as those commonly used in service learning lessons and project-based instruction. Have one teaching team facilitate learning while the other team meets. Then switch roles.

Make It Special

Ask special subject teachers if it is possible to schedule your students at times that will help you optimize your planning minutes. For example, having back-to-back special area classes once per week can help teachers in elementary and middle school gain extended planning time. Paraprofessionals may even be able to participate in these meetings if some of your students with disabilities occasionally do not need support during particular lessons or units.

Repurpose Time

If additional resources are not available, structural changes can be made to existing schedules to create or repurpose time for meetings. For instance, one middle school we visited had daily grade level team planning. When they started a co-teaching model, they began using one of those team meetings as "diverse learner" planning sessions. This became a time for co-teaching teams to break off into their own separate meetings. It also gave all teachers time to connect with therapists, counselors, parents and others who could help all students succeed.

Plan With, Not For

Some schools have taken planning to their students and have involved them in some of the process. Teachers might share upcoming units and ask learners to give input on learning experiences, instructional materials and even on strategies for meeting goals. This type of exercise can't replace regular planning, of course, but it can shorten the formal time teachers need to spend on the task and it can drastically increase student buy-in and interest in both teaching and learning.

Staff Shuffle

Look for inventive ways to shuffle staff and resources to meet your co-planning goals. You might find ways to work creatively with teachers in other grades (think multi-age experiences), with administrators, with student teachers or with counselors and social workers. Do you have a principal who occasionally likes to read to your students or teach a lesson? If so, use this time for an impromptu meeting. Does your counselor want more time in classrooms to talk about social topics like bullying, peer support and coping techniques? Invite him in and open your plan books.

Or propose a larger shuffling of roles and responsibilities. In one school, special studies days were created where the art teacher, music teacher and two paraprofessionals collaborated to teach an entire grade level (sixty-five students) for ninety minutes at a time. Students loved the chance to engage in the unique cross-curricular projects (e.g., one-act plays, mosaics, song writing competitions) developed by the teaching team, and teachers loved the extra time to plan. To make the arrangement fair and to ensure the lessons were high-quality, the music teacher and the art teacher were also given designated planning time.

Stand By Your Man (Or Woman)

Plan a series of stand-up meetings with your partner. This type of meeting is becoming very popular in corporate America and is commonly used to set goals and review action items. During these meetings, both or all participants stand and meetings are kept to a few topics and a strict fifteen-minute time limit.

Walk & Talk

How about meeting while you exercise? Okay, that might be a stretch (pun intended) for those who think a bit more "in the box," but if you both have an interest in running, walking, kickboxing or pumping iron, why not take your planning to the track, court, ring or pool? We love this option because you can "knock out" (get it?) your professional and personal goals at the same time.

Ten Minutes At A Time

Are you really desperate? Try breaking your meetings into ten-minute segments. Fitness experts will tell you that thirty minutes of daily exercise does not need to be done in one fell swoop. You can meet this goal by running or walking for ten minutes, three times a day. This same philosophy can be applied to team meetings. While not ideal, you may need to choose several days a week to meet and find ten minutes during each one of them. Remember to be focused and set a clear mini-goal for each tiny meeting.

Dance Meeting

Okay, we are kidding but wanted to see if you were still paying attention. Wait! Really? This is your favorite idea? Then turn up the music, start to hustle, twist or shuffle and get down to planning.

Designing Face-To-Face Alternatives & Add-Ons

Still don't have all the time you need? Don't panic. Well, go ahead and panic a little but then stop. It will be okay. Some of the most successful teams we know are the ones that have figured out an efficient method of communication, even when they don't have much face-to-face time together. We have seen all of these methods work successfully. The trick is finding systems that work for both of you, assessing them throughout the year and revising when necessary.

Communication Notebooks

Establish a communication notebook that all members of the team can read and respond to regularly. Use your notebook to record questions, changes in schedules or child-specific information. Use good old fashioned paper and pencil or explore an app like *Simplenote* (by Automattic) to make notes easier to access across people and environments.

Mailboxes

Designate a mailbox in the classroom for each staff member where any notes or materials (e.g., teaching props, assessment tools) can be placed and retrieved.

Texts

Texts or e-mails can be used as supplements to other methods of communication. Electronic communication may not be the best choice for sharing detailed information but using it is better than not having access to your partner at all. Texts and e-mails are especially helpful if you need to share last-minute questions (J need modified test 2day?), comments (10Q 4 finishing the b-board) or scheduling changes (still in advisory—can't meet…reschedule?). And keep in mind that texting is a great excuse to use all of those adorable emojis on your phone, including those that seem specifically designed for co-teacher communication:

Lesson Plans

Lesson plans themselves can be a great tool for communication if they are physically or virtually available at all times and if both of you agree that you will use them in this way. If you like using your plans to supplement formal planning time, be sure that you both understand how you will share comments, provide feedback and add new content. You might, for instance, each be responsible for creating a certain number of plans each week and for commenting on your partner's drafts by the time you sit down to meet face-to-face.

SKYPE

Can't find time to meet at school? Some teams may find it easier to meet long after the bell rings when they are cozy on their couches at home. Virtual meetings are not for everyone, we admit, but for those that have challenging schedules (think running to graduate school classes after school or coaching extra-curricular activities), cyberspace may be the most comfortable and ideal place to get together. So, pick up the phone if you like this option, or switch over to Skype or FaceTime so you can create fabulous plans while showing off your extra-fuzzy footie pajamas.

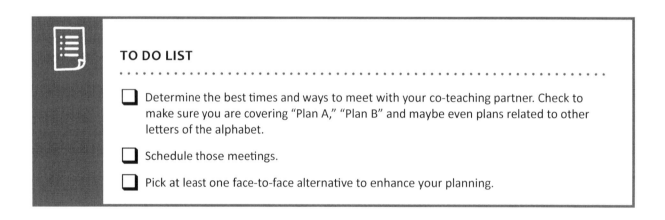

TO DO LIST

☐ Determine the best times and ways to meet with your co-teaching partner. Check to make sure you are covering "Plan A," "Plan B" and maybe even plans related to other letters of the alphabet.

☐ Schedule those meetings.

☐ Pick at least one face-to-face alternative to enhance your planning.

PLAN TO PLAN

So, you have found time to plan, right? Well, not oodles and oodles of time, but some? We certainly hope so. No matter how much time you have, however, if you are like most co-teaching teams, you constantly have to do more with less. For this reason, we have come up with a set of tools that will help every team experience the best possible planning meetings.

On Day 6, we will look at two "musts" for your planning. You must find an ideal environment and you must amass the right tools. You must!

Environment

Planning to plan always starts with finding the best meeting space. While this is usually the classroom, it doesn't have to be. You should choose a spot that makes you feel most productive and one that allows you to best focus on the task at hand. If that happens to be a conference room, meet there, but if you get more done hanging out at your favorite taco truck, who are we to argue? Possible meeting sites include your playground jungle gym, the school library, the empty auditorium, a favorite restaurant or a somewhat-favorite restaurant that is less expensive than your favorite restaurant.

Tools

Any effective co-planning duo needs an amazing collection of tools for meetings. This collection includes but is not limited to:

⚒ Meeting Guidelines

Whether you are meeting as a pair or as a larger team, you need a list of meeting guidelines. This list should be thoughtfully assembled. That is, you don't need to include every possible rule of conduct, just a few essentials that will make your meetings efficient and effective. Your list should be (a) short and to the point, (b) displayed each and every meeting and (c) eventually memorized and internalized by every member of the team.

Sample guidelines include:

- *We always begin and end on time.*
- *We honor time limits.*
- *Everyone participates—we start and end each meeting by going around the table to hear from each member of the team.*
- *We listen to understand.*
- *We don't interrupt—one person speaks at a time.*
- *We are honest.*
- *Our meetings are positive and upbeat.*
- *We are present (no phones/computers/tablets except for planning purposes).*
- *We are brief when voicing our opinions.*
- *We always end with actions/task review.*

We recommend framing your guidelines and hanging them in your space or at least laminating them and hauling them out for each meeting. See Figure 6.1 for a set of guidelines created by a team of Kindergarten co-teachers.

FIGURE 6.1
Team Meeting Guidelines: Example

- ☐ We start and end on time.
- ☐ We use our phones for planning and research purposes only (no unnecessary texting/calls).
- ☐ We rotate roles and responsibilities; we take turns facilitating.
- ☐ We stick to the agenda.

- ☐ We always share at least one Kindergarten success story!
- ☐ We accept and welcome constructive criticism.
- ☐ One person talks at a time.
- ☐ We regularly reflect on our process and stick to these guidelines.

⚒ Agenda

Don't even bother meeting without an agenda. The agenda is the centerpiece of your team meetings. It dictates which items you need to discuss, how long you need to discuss them and, possibly, who will be presenting them to the group. Not sure where to get an agenda? Don't worry, we will provide you with an easy-to-use format on Day 8. Go ahead and peek if you must. We'll wait.

⚒ Role Cards

No matter how big or small your meetings, be sure to regularly rotate roles, so that no one person is always in charge and every member has opportunities to polish collaborative skills (e.g., managing time, facilitating meetings). The easiest way to remember to switch things up is to create role cards (see Figure 6.2) and distribute them at each meeting. Even if you are only meeting with one other person, you will want to use your cards or at least remember to adopt specific roles. For two of you, you might simply have one facilitator and one recorder. If you have a larger planning team, you can expand to other roles, such as observer, time keeper and encourager. But wait...there's more! Keep adding to the roles you use until you find your favorites. How about trying out lavish praise distributor, guidelines guru, fun one, photographer/documentarian or caterer?

We encourage you to be creative with roles and assign responsibilities that work best for your group, but there are a few roles we do not recommend. These include snorter/eye roller, passive observer, arguer, insulter, naysayer or the "I've tried that and it won't work" repeater.

Do-Not-Disturb Sign

Hang a "we are planning-do not disturb" sign on the door during your meetings. We are not kidding about this—it is an almost-surefire way to head off colleagues who have a new Internet joke to share, administrators who want to talk about chaperones for the class trip to the fish hatchery or students who want to look for a missing sweatshirt "one more time." See Figure 6.3 for a sign that you can print and use immediately.

 Chart Paper & Markers

Keep some paper on the wall to take notes, "park" topics that come up but can't be addressed in the meeting or play a quick game of hangman with your co-teaching partner (but only if it is on the agenda).

IMPLEMENTATION TIP

Want to move additional notes, topic "parking" and hangman games from chart paper to your tablet? Try an app like *Flipink* (by huang xiang) to experiment with sketchnoting and graphic facilitation during your meetings.

 Timer

The timer is used to keep your meeting running smoothly and to ensure that your team or group stays focused, refrains from off-topic comments and conversations and covers the targeted agenda items. Set the timer for an agreed upon number of minutes as you discuss each item on the agenda and let it serve as a signal to change topics. The timer should also be used to end the meeting on time.

Food

Healthy snacks are fine, but if you want to sweet talk your co-teaching partner into helping you design a new unit or taking on the lion's share of grading quizzes, we suggest bringing chocolate or something else irresistible like bacon, or you might want to just cover all the bases with chocolate-covered bacon.

IMPLEMENTATION TIP

. . . .

Use an empty locker near your meeting location to store all of your tools. One team we know posts the weekly agenda on the inside of their locker and team members stop by and add to the agenda throughout the week.

TO DO LIST

. . . .

☐ Determine the best environment for your meetings.

☐ Create meeting guidelines. Commit them to memory. Know them. Live them. Recite them in your sleep.

☐ Commit to using an agenda. Pinkie swear that you will.

☐ Make some role cards that will be the envy of your grade level or academic department.

☐ Print the do-not-disturb sign, laminate it and hang it.

☐ Gather some chart paper. Consider it a bonus if you can find the kind with the sticky stuff on the back.

☐ Get a timer.

☐ Start stockpiling snacks.

☐ Gather any other essential tools and find a place to keep them all.

FIGURE 6.2
Team Meeting Role Cards

Print this page. Cut out your cards and use them during meetings to learn about team meeting roles.

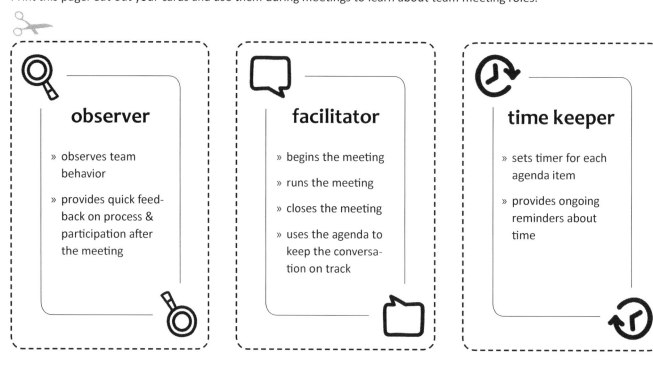

observer

- » observes team behavior
- » provides quick feedback on process & participation after the meeting

facilitator

- » begins the meeting
- » runs the meeting
- » closes the meeting
- » uses the agenda to keep the conversation on track

time keeper

- » sets timer for each agenda item
- » provides ongoing reminders about time

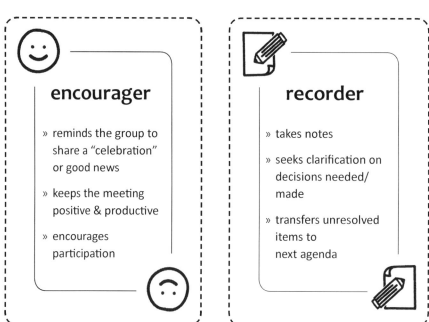

encourager

- » reminds the group to share a "celebration" or good news
- » keeps the meeting positive & productive
- » encourages participation

recorder

- » takes notes
- » seeks clarification on decisions needed/ made
- » transfers unresolved items to next agenda

*inspired by the work of Allison Ford (1995) & The Wisconsin School Inclusion Project

FIGURE 6.3
Do-Not-Disturb Sign

Copy this page on thick paper and laminate. Then, punch holes in the two upper corners of the sign, string twine or ribbon through the holes and tie knots to secure. Hang it on your door for every single meeting.

PLEASE DO NOT DISTURB

Don't be jealous, but we are having a mind-blowing, highly effective & incredibly efficient team meeting. Feel free to come back when we finish at

_____ .

Who knows? We may have extra snacks!

DAY 7

MAKE MEETINGS MATTER

Most of us have been to meetings that are inefficiently run. You will know you are in one of those types of meetings when you:

» *start to alphabetize things in your head*
» *want to poke out your own eye with a pencil*
» *want to poke out somebody else's eye with a pencil*
» *keep opening your mouth to silently scream*
» *become enraged and begin to berate yourself mentally for attending the meeting*
» *create an elaborate list of to-do items written in calligraphy and color coded*
» *draw pictures of the other people at the meeting on your scratch paper and begin to add cool hats*
» *suddenly remember you had to make a dentist appointment and leap up to do that*
» *check your Facebook page and update your status with phrases like, "help me" or "get me outta here"*

We realize that we have possibly just given you an unpleasant flashback to your last meeting and we apologize. Fortunately, we are going to redeem ourselves by sharing ideas for running the best meetings possible. Let's go to a better place, shall we?

We Have To Start Meeting Like This

Both of us consider ourselves to be pretty laid back in most areas of our lives. We seldom make our beds and usually plan our vacations by heading to the airport and asking the ticket agent, "Where do you think we should go?" This relaxed attitude, however, stops at the meeting table. We may not care if we lay on a beach in Boca or go to a dude ranch in Durango, but we do care about efficiently run meetings. For this reason, we recommend that teachers use the same systematic process to run their meetings week in and week out. It can feel strange at first to follow steps that may seem fairly rigid, but if you can get accustomed to this process and even embrace it, you will find that your meetings are more effective, your participants are less frustrated and you become so addicted to using timers that you just timed how long it took you to read this paragraph. Here are the steps:

1. Write It Down

Assign a recorder and have that person take minutes; this can be done using a hard copy of a meeting form or a virtual tool. Every part of the meeting does not need to be recorded, but you will need to capture main points of the discussion and any decisions that are made. If the agenda item requires one or more members of the team to take action, get information, make a contact or create materials, those specific tasks should be very clearly outlined.

2. Check In

Set your timer for five minutes for the first agenda item. This should be your check-in.

In this short period of time you need to go back to the minutes from your last meeting and review tasks that were to be accomplished between then and now (e.g., "Sheila, you were going to design new communication board templates for our inventions unit for Trevor. Did you finish?"; "Howard, you were working on planning the ecology service learning project. Did you find a community mentor for us?"). Then, transfer any items from your old agenda to your new agenda such as any tasks that have not been completed or topics that still need more discussion. In the best-case scenario, you have been developing your new agenda since your last meeting and now have before you the most pressing items. At this time you will review your list and add anything that didn't make the agenda but should have. Then, assign each item an appropriate segment of time (e.g., five minutes for items that require only a quick decision and twenty minutes for discussing the outline of an upcoming unit).

As you fine-tune your agenda, keep in mind this process may also involve deleting content. Before you move on to the next step, determine if you have enough time for all the slated items and remove anything that may not be important enough for a sit-down meeting or at least for this one.

3. Celebrate

When possible, share good news as part of your check-in. If your team is skilled at running efficient meetings, this should only take about one or two minutes, but set the timer to be sure it doesn't go on much longer.

You can generate the good news collaboratively or go around the table and have each person share a quick "celebration" (e.g., "Kyle completed three days of homework"; "Tyler used a new app to answer three comprehension questions last week").

4. Get Down To Business

Set the timer again to tackle your first item of business. Be sure to be concise in your discussion and fairly quick with your decision-making. If you find you cannot make a decision or discuss the issue in the time provided, you will either need to propose extending the time provided (and agree to shorten or delete another topic) or move the discussion or decision to your next meeting.

5. Keep It Moving

Continue this process as you move down the agenda. As you address each topic, be mindful not only of the discussion you are having but also of the meeting itself. Is everyone being productive? Are you following the agenda? Are people communicating effectively? Are your guidelines being followed? If you find your team needs any help keeping the energy up and the topics flowing, check out our list of power phrases in Table 7.1. These suggestions can go a long way toward keeping meetings focused.

6. Wrap It Up

We recommend that the last five to ten minutes of the meeting be used as the "wrap-up and review." When you get to this agenda item, you (a) decide which topics need to be transferred to the next agenda because they are unresolved, need to be visited again or require more steps and (b) review who needs to do what before the next meeting. If you skip this step, expect your meetings to lack clarity, focus and direction. Repeating this process at the end of each gathering provides some insurance that your hard work will result in progress and results.

7. End With Energy

In the beginning of your meeting, you shared something positive about the week. At the end of the meeting, you should also share something positive. This time, however, you will focus on something positive about the meeting itself. Share one or two positive reflections (e.g., "This team rocks! We were so efficient with our discussion of report cards!"; "Thanks to Kelly for keeping us on track"). This final step will make your meetings more enjoyable and help the team focus on good news and positive communication.

We Have To Keep Meeting Like This

Repeat these steps at every meeting. Not at some meetings. Not at most meetings. At every single one.

If you stay disciplined and use this process regularly, you will find you are accomplishing more and becoming fluent in a whole range of collaborative skills. Skeptical? Need more help? Check out our "Meeting Dos & Don'ts" in Table 7.2. You are sure to find inspiration in this list of remedies.

Can you feel that? You are quickly becoming meeting masters. Take a team bow.

TO DO LIST

- ☐ Try the process one time through and evaluate when you finish. Was it hard to follow the steps? Did you take meaningful notes? Did you end on time?
- ☐ Talk about improvements you can make so that your meetings become more effective and efficient.
- ☐ Practice your power phrases. Develop your own. Use them on strangers at the mall as in, "Thanks for ringing me up, but let's quickly check our watches before we do anything else so we can be sure to end this transaction on time."
- ☐ Teach the team meeting process to someone else.

TABLE 7.1
Power Phrases for Positive & Productive Meetings

TO START THE MEETING

"I love meetings! Let's get started."

"Set that timer. Let's get going. Yes. Really. Set the timer."

"What time do we need to finish? Let's be conscious of the clock throughout the meeting so that we are done on time."

"Let's briefly review the agenda together."

"Let's briefly review where we left off last week and provide updates on any tasks that were assigned."

"Wow! Our guidelines are fabulous. Let's review them before we get started."

"What are we celebrating today?"

TO STAY ON TRACK

"Let's get back to the agenda."

"Let's go around and hear from everyone on this issue before moving to the next."

"Let's quickly check the time before we move on."

"Record that so we can use it/act on it/meet about it later."

"So far, we have covered _____ and _____. Let's move to the next item on the agenda."

"Put that in the 'parking lot' so we can discuss it later."

TO KEEP MEMBERS FROM GETTING "STUCK"

"What's stopping us from making a decision?"

"You/some of us seem to be bored/confused/upset/ sleeping. What's happening?"

"Should we ask _____ to get us more information before we make a decision?"

"I think this is a decision for _____. Shall we ask him/her to make it?"

"This conversation seems a bit off topic. Let's table it and come back to it at the end of the meeting if we have time."

TO CLOSE THE MEETING

"This meeting was epic. I can't wait to do it again."

"Have I told you lately how much I enjoy these meetings?"

"What decisions have we made?"

"Who will do what by when?"

"How and when will these decisions be shared with other stakeholders?"

"What are the next steps?"

"How did we do? What went well in this meeting?"

TABLE 7.2

Co-Teaching Meeting Dos & Don'ts

Dos	 Don'ts
Hang a do-not-disturb sign on your door to avoid interruptions.	Invite any and all passersby into the meeting for food, fun and conversation.
Be on time.	Show up late, leave early and offer to be the meeting's timekeeper.
Stay focused.	Take some selfies. Make dollar bill origami sculptures. Try to remember all the names of the Von Trapp family singers.
Use an agenda.	Randomly discuss topics as they pop into your head or draw your discussion items from the copies of the *People* magazine laying on your desk.
Set a time limit for each agenda item.	Talk about each item until you are mentally and physically exhausted or until the meeting ends--whichever comes first.
Keep meeting minutes. Review them at each meeting.	Try to remember some of what was said and most of the tasks assigned.
Occasionally bring refreshments.	Give your co-teacher half of the snickerdoodle you brought for lunch. Then, spend a significant amount of time either talking about where you got the recipe for snickerdoodles you brought or interrupting her to ask if she likes them more or less or as much as her grandmother's snickerdoodles.
Stay positive.	Complain about students, parents, the administration, the weather, any back pain you have, traffic, the overabundance of zombie movies being produced, corn syrup and pop-up ads on YouTube.
End on time.	Continue to meet indefinitely, ignoring natural cues like the custodian turning out the lights or the glare of the midnight moon.

TAKE NOTE

Feeling overwhelmed yet? We are here to help. The step-by-step process outlined on Day 7 can be easily mastered. It takes just a bit of practice and a detailed notetaking format that will guide you through each step of your meeting. Not sure where to get such a comprehensive tool? Not to worry. We have created one for you to fill out with your team. You're welcome. No really. Stop that. You are embarrassing us. It was nothing.

In this section of the book, we will explain each piece of this notetaking form (see Figure 8.1 for a blank template and Figure 8.2 for a sample set of notes). We will not only take you through the basic tasks, such as listing agenda items and determining action items, but will also introduce you to the "bling" of this form—the soundtrack, movie quote and celebration section.

The Basics

If you don't want to use the form we have created for you, you can certainly find or design your own. No matter what tool, template or format you use, however, we recommend you include a few basic elements. Sections we recommend include agenda items (description and type), time required, action required, person responsible and timeline.

Agenda Items

The first part of filling in your form involves listing your agenda items. In the first column on the left-hand side, simply record each topic that you plan to cover during the meeting.

It's best to form your agenda on an ongoing basis. In other words, the entire list should not be created as you sit down to meet. Items should come from (a) content you did not cover at your last meeting; (b) issues that have come up since your last meeting that require discussion and decision-making; and (c) anything new you feel you need to add as you sit down to meet.

Types Of Agenda Items

Don't skip this column. Take just a moment to "code" each agenda item. Does it require a discussion? Is it there because a decision needs to be made? Is it an important point to celebrate? Or are you sharing it with your co-teacher to keep yourself from blowing a gasket (e.g., "You need to laugh harder at my metric system knock-knock jokes")? This step will save you time and serve as a reminder that agenda items should not be treated equally. If an item is there as a reminder only, it should not be discussed.

Time Required

This is another "must" on your meeting form. The time-keeper needs estimates to keep the meeting on track. This task can be a challenge initially, but over time you will get better at assessing the number of minutes required for certain types of agenda items. Start by overestimating so that you will not be frustrated by the pace of your initial meetings.

Action Required

Now it's time to get down to business. This part of the form prompts you to determine which action or actions are required as a result of your meeting. Has someone been assigned to create materials? Does one of you need to talk to an administrator, call a parent or communicate with a therapist? Do you both have research to do for upcoming units? All of those activities would need to be listed in the "action required" column. It is important to not only list each action, but to do so in detail. In other words, "Do that one thing we said," may not be quite enough.

Person Responsible

The next column is pretty self-explanatory. You now know what needs to happen. Assign those tasks! Keep in mind, of course, that you may be able to delegate some of the tasks on your list. Look at each item and determine if any of the work can and should be done by a collaborative partner who is not at the meeting (e.g., administrator), a paraprofessional on your team, a classroom volunteer or even a student.

Timeline

Last but not least is the timeline. You must be very clear about the "when" of your required actions. Set reasonable targets and list the date the actions will be completed. Feel free to be ultra-specific, as in "by Thursday, November 11, at the beginning of our meeting."

IMPLEMENTATION TIP

Want to go paperless? Use Google Docs to take notes and make them accessible to your team and try an app like *Agenda Maker* (from ydangle) to organize your meeting topics.

The Bling

Okay, so now it's time for the really important stuff. Let's take a look at the elements that will make your planning form shine. Read on to learn about soundtrack suggestions, movie quotes and celebrations.

Soundtrack Suggestion

If it isn't obvious why your notetaking form needs a soundtrack suggestion, then you are not bringing your funkiest self to the reading of this book. We like the soundtrack idea because, well…let's face it, some meetings just need tunes. Any song can be the soundtrack for your meeting, but we suggest matching the mood and needs of the team with your musical choices. Everyone feeling excited about the new year? Try "Happy" by Pharrell Williams. Sleepy from a long night of grading projects? Pop in "Wake Up" by Arcade Fire. Planning the middle school trip to Washington, DC? Consider "I Will Survive" by Gloria Gaynor.

Movie Quote

If we have convinced you to add a soundtrack to your notes, might we also get you to extend the fun and choose a relevant movie quote? We know you might be apprehensive at first, but once you have started framing your meetings with movie quotes, we bet you won't be able to have even a short conversation without imitating Jennifer Lawrence, Samuel L. Jackson or Will Ferrell.

Curious about what to choose? We have ideas. Have a big IEP meeting or student evaluation coming up? Try, "Here's looking at you at you, kid!" New class lists coming out? Consider, "Life is like a box of chocolates. You never know what you are going to get." Last week of school? May we suggest, "Hasta la vista, baby!"

Celebration

Even if you don't fill out the song suggestion and movie quote section for each meeting (unthinkable, but it might happen from time to time), we do hope you pay attention to celebrating at least one achievement, realization, lesson, moment or person every time you plan. It doesn't take much time, but it can pay large dividends in awareness and motivation. And now that we are thinking about it, consider using "Celebration" by Kool and the Gang for your soundtrack choice every now and then; not only is it a great jam, but it will allow you to bump, hustle and boogaloo to all of the good news you have to share.

TO DO LIST

- [ ] Review the team meeting notes form with your co-teacher. Discuss helpful aspects or potential changes. Then, decide to either adopt the form or design your own form.

- [ ] Make a team meeting soundtrack filled with different songs you can play for different types of meetings (e.g., after-school, multi-hour). Try not to break out your best dance moves during the actual meeting.

- [ ] Search for a few great go-to movie quotes to kick off or end your plan time. Practice using these quotes not only in your meetings but across the school day to secretly communicate with your partner. Use different accents. Keep speaking in movie quotes, slowly replacing most of your utterances with movie quotes. Repeat this recommendation until one of you can't take it anymore.

- [ ] Start to pay attention to all there is to celebrate throughout the day and across each week. Be ready to share one or more accomplishments at each meeting.

FIGURE 8.1

Team Meeting Notes

Soundtrack: _____

We are celebrating: _____

Movie quote that captures the spirit of our work this week: _____

AGENDA ITEMS	TYPE OF AGENDA ITEM FYI: Information JD: Just Discussion ND: Needs Decision JWB: Just Want To Brag NTGOMCBIE: Need To Get Off My Chest Before I Explode	TIME REQUIRED (e.g., 5 minutes, an hour)	ACTION/S REQUIRED (e.g., make materials, research topic, create adaptations, look for a volunteer)	PERSON/S RESPONSIBLE (e.g., pod 2 team, Reed & Jay)	TIMELINE (e.g., by next week)
		☐ 5 min ☐ 10 min ☐ ____			
		☐ 5 min ☐ 10 min ☐ ____			
		☐ 5 min ☐ 10 min ☐ ____			
		☐ 5 min ☐ 10 min ☐ ____			
		☐ 5 min ☐ 10 min ☐ ____			

Adapted from: Ford, A. (1995). Wisconsin School Inclusion Project: A Team Planning Packet for Inclusive Education.

FIGURE 8.2
Team Meeting Notes: Example

 Soundtrack:

"We Are All Accelerated Readers" by Los Campesinos!

We are celebrating:

Students have already read 100 books this year.

Movie quote that captures the spirit of our work this week:

"I want my two dollars!" - Better Off Dead

AGENDA ITEMS	TYPE OF AGENDA ITEM FYI: Information JD: Just Discussion ND: Needs Decision JWB: Just Want To Brag NTGOMCBIE: Need To Get Off My Chest Before I Explode	TIME REQUIRED (e.g., 5 minutes, an hour)	ACTION/S REQUIRED (e.g., make materials, research topic, create adaptations, look for a volunteer)	PERSON/S RESPONSIBLE (e.g., pod 2 team, Reed & Jay)	TIMELINE (e.g., by next week)
intro lesson for *Walk Two Moons*	ND	☐ 5 min ☑ 10 min ✓20	• Assemble presentation for "special message" (e.g., "Don't judge a man until you've walked two moons in his moccasins") mini-movies.	Wendy	start of school day- 11/1
lit partners: pairings & selections	ND	☐ 5 min ☑ 10 min ✓10	• Create rubric.	Victoria	start of school day- 11/1
			• Share with students tomorrow.	both of us	tomorrow during language arts
fieldtrip $ (need $2.00/student)	FYI	☐ 5 min ☑ 10 min ✓	• Put one more announcement on blog.	Victoria	by 3:00 today
Tara's IEP progress	JWB	☐ 5 min ☑ 10 min ✓	n/a	n/a	n/a
		☐ 5 min ☐ 10 min ☐			

Adapted from: Ford, A. (1995). Wisconsin School Inclusion Project: A Team Planning Packet for Inclusive Education.

NAME YOUR NORMS

You have the structure of your meetings set so it's time to focus on what you do or say in those meetings. That is, it's time to set collaboration norms. Norms are essentially a set of behavior guidelines or agreements that members of a team use to run meetings effectively and efficiently. Collaboration norms can also help co-teaching teams establish a culture that is positive and cooperative, as the norms serve as tools for listening and sharing, and as reminders to be respectful, open and willing to work together.

Seven Norms Of Collaboration

Teams can invent their own norms, adopt a set of norms created by colleagues or adopt a formal collaboration model. We typically suggest the latter for new teams and most often recommend the "seven norms of collaboration" from the work of Bill Baker (as cited in Garmston & Wellman, 1999). These norms were created as a result of Baker's observation that it was not enough for facilitators to have high-quality collaboration skills. He felt that meetings would be much more effective if all members also had a working knowledge of best practices in listening and sharing ideas. The seven norms he proposed are pausing, paraphrasing, probing for specificity, putting ideas on the table, paying attention to self and others, presuming positive intentions and pursuing a balance between advocacy and inquiry. Each one is explored in detail in this section and, yes, each one starts with a P—isn't that peculiar? And perfect? And pleasing?

Pausing

Pausing before responding or asking a question allows time for thinking and enhances dialogue, discussion and decision-making. You and your partner may not have brains that fire at the same rate or in the same way. In fact, it is likely you do not. Pausing can help both of you stay apace during a rich discussion and can communicate that you are committed to being thoughtful in your remarks during formal meeting time. There are several different types of pauses. You can use spontaneous or structured collective pauses to give your team a moment to think before commenting on an issue or point. You can also use pausing to create personal reflection time; this time can be used to think, take notes or examine something in writing. Finally, you can pause after a question or after someone speaks to provide a space for team members to create the most thoughtful responses possible. Let's practice. Pause. Okay. Move on.

Paraphrasing

Paraphrasing is a powerful way to indicate that you are listening to others, honoring their contributions and trying your best to understand them. As you paraphrase, try to maintain both the intention and the accuracy of what your communication partner has shared. Further, avoid using "I" as you rephrase your colleague's message.

When paraphrasing, try using phrases like:

> » *You want to know if ...*
> » *You are suggesting that ...*
> » *You are worried that ...*
> » *You are unsure of ...*
> » *So, you are beginning to wonder if ...*
> » *You feel nervous about ...*
> » *You need more information about ...*
> » *You are all thinking that we should ...*

Probing For Specificity

Probing is a tool that can help teams drill down into specifics and address important details. It can help participants move away from communication barriers like generalizations and distortions. Probing can also help team members think about their language and word choices. For example, your co-teaching partner may think that when you say you will "take care of the volunteers" for the entrepreneur unit, you are going to find three volunteers, train them and schedule them for upcoming activities. If she probes further, however, she may learn that you only meant you would create an ad for the classroom newsletter and find some likely candidates.

Probes are intended to "battle" vague nouns and pronouns such as "they," "him" and "boys with learning disabilities " (e.g., "They just cannot pay attention"); vague action words such as "plan," "create," "develop" and "support" (e.g., "We should support Dan more effectively"); comparators like "best," "slower" and "more" (e.g., "Second period students are much more motivated than fourth period students"); rule words like "can't," "shouldn't" and "must" (e.g., "We should not give students adapted seating unless they have identified needs "); and universal qualifiers like "never," "always" and "all" (e.g., "All testing must take place in this room").

Vague language can cause misunderstandings in meetings and in daily communication, so it is important that both or all team members know how to probe for more information when they hear it. When one co-teacher says, "They just don't study," the other might follow that comment with, "When you say 'they' do you mean the students who failed, the four students with disabilities or Tamika and Ray? Which students do you think are not studying?"

To probe for specificity, try using open-ended prompts like:

> » *Please say more about …*
> » *Elaborate about …*
> » *I want to better understand what you said about …*
> » *I'd like to hear more about …*
> » *Are you saying …*
> » *Keep talking. I want to be sure I understand your concern.*
> » *You said _____. Can you give me an example of that?*
> » *You said _____. What did you mean by that?*

Putting Ideas On The Table

Co-teaching partners should feel comfortable sharing ideas with one another as they brainstorm, problem solve and plan. Flexibility is absolutely key in this process. Participants should be open-minded as they both offer ideas and field them. One way to demonstrate such tractability is to use language that communicates an understanding that offering ideas is not the same as making a decision.

Phrases that will help you and your partner "put ideas on the table" include:

> » *One idea to consider is …*
> » *A possible approach would be to …*
> » *I'm just thinking out loud as I say this, but how about …*
> » *This might sound a little odd, but what if we tried to …*
> » *Have we thought about …*
> » *When I say _____, what comes to mind?*

Paying Attention To Self & Others

Every co-teacher will likely have different preferences, needs and habits when it comes to communicating and planning. Whenever possible, adapt your own communication style to make your partner feel comfortable and supported. When you interact with your partner, pay attention to her words, body language and learning style. Then, use your observations to interact in a way that you feel your partner will appreciate and understand. For instance, if you notice that your partner needs you to be direct, get right to the point and use clear language and examples. If she learns visually, provide data sheets when you discuss student progress. If he is always on time and takes copious notes, you might take this as a cue that he is a person who values precision and may like to conduct meetings in a fairly formal fashion.

Paying attention to self and others also involves the constant consideration of how your own behavior is affecting the group. Are you talking too much? Not offering enough? Entering the room with a not-so-great attitude? Sharing anecdotes of your newborn baby in between every agenda item during your Friday afternoon meeting? All of these considerations need attention from each and every group member.

Presuming Positive Intentions

Maybe it seems obvious that co-teaching partners should work from a positive point of view and that they should assume that others' intentions are positive, but we feel it cannot hurt to reinforce a norm that is this important. This tenet promotes and facilitates meaningful dialogue and discussion and prevents unintentional putdowns. Presuming positive intentions means that even when tensions may run high, team members try to operate from a space of respect and curiosity. For example, if your occupational therapist expresses discomfort about teaching in your co-taught inclusive classroom by saying, "I wish I could just pull these students into my office. I don't really know how to support Jim during Writers' Workshop," assume that he is a professional who wants to do the right thing for students. You don't want to jump down his throat and scream, "You hate inclusive schooling! We knew you would resist this fabulous opportunity to collaborate!" Instead, you might say, "As a therapist, I know you want Jim to gain new skills this year and be successful in this new environment. What kinds of activities do you usually engage in when you are in the OT room? What are some of the barriers to working in the classroom? How can we, as Jim's teachers, help to figure this out?"

Using positive intentions in speech is one manifestation of this norm. Team members presuming positive intentions should adopt phrases such as:

- » *I can hear that you are coming from a place of concern/interest …*
- » *It's obvious we both/all have a shared goal of …*
- » *I appreciate what you are saying …*
- » *What you are saying makes sense because …*
- » *Thank you for mentioning that because …*

Pursuing A Balance Between Advocacy & Inquiry

This last norm is based on the work of Peter Senge (2006) and is useful for our work with colleagues, as well as with students and families. Pursuing a balance between advocacy and inquiry means simply that each collaborative partner should demonstrate a willingness to get and give input, to listen and to act.

Inquiry provides for greater understanding. Advocacy leads to decision-making. One of the common mistakes that collaborative teams may make is to bring closure to problem identification (inquiry for understanding) too quickly and rush into resolving that problem (advocacy for a specific solution). Maintaining a balance between advocating for a position and inquiring about the position can help teams or co-teaching partners find the best possible solution instead of just finding a solution.

Using The Norms

Like any new skill or behavior that has to be learned, these seven norms require practice and conscious attention. Individuals using them for the first time may find the process awkward. With some practice, however, most co-teaching teams find that the norms not only feel relatively easy to use, but hard to live without. You may find you have the desire to needlepoint them on a pillow or tattoo them on your forearm. If you are not that crafty or edgy, you might just print this section of the book and keep it with your planning materials.

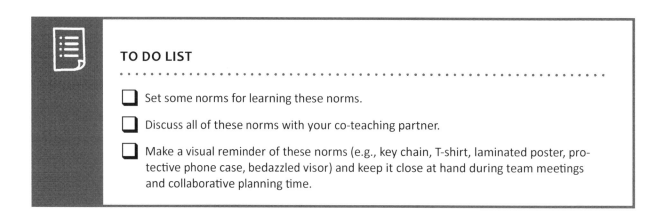

TO DO LIST

☐ Set some norms for learning these norms.

☐ Discuss all of these norms with your co-teaching partner.

☐ Make a visual reminder of these norms (e.g., key chain, T-shirt, laminated poster, protective phone case, bedazzled visor) and keep it close at hand during team meetings and collaborative planning time.

OPERATE AS EQUALS

How do you know co-teachers have yet to establish themselves as true partners in the eyes of students, colleagues or other stakeholders? There are actually many telltale signs. Here are a few:

» *Parents only know one of the teachers.*
» *One teacher calls the space "my classroom" instead of "our classroom."*
» *One teacher repeatedly asks the other for "license, registration or other ID" as he or she enters the classroom.*
» *Students talk about one of their co-teachers as their "real" teacher and regularly refer to the other one as "the other one."*
» *There are rumors circulating that one co-teacher is an administrative spy.*
» *Students regularly tell one of their teachers, "My parents told me not to talk to strangers."*
» *One teacher has a desk in front of the classroom and the other has a desk in the back corner or in the hallway or wait...that teacher has no desk at all.*
» *One teacher is primarily positioned at the front of the classroom and one is primarily positioned to the side or at the back of the classroom.*
» *One teacher is primarily positioned at the front of the classroom while the other "crouch walks" around the classroom, whispering to students. This teacher has occasionally been asked by his or her co-teaching partner to "keep it down."*

> » *One teacher is primarily positioned at the front of the classroom and the other can be found wandering the hallways, getting coffee or Tweeting about the need to establish equity in the classroom.*

IMPLEMENTATION TIP

Not sure how students view your team? Consider: "What evidence do we have that students see us as equals? Do we have any evidence that they do not see us as equals?" Have an open conversation about these questions with your co-teacher.

Sometimes these behaviors are signs of tension in a co-teaching relationship, but other times, co-teachers are just unaware of the importance of "showing off" their shared commitment and reinventing classroom roles in their new situation. To avoid the pitfalls above, Cook and Friend (1995) suggest that adults working together in schools send parity signals to communicate their cooperation to others. Parity signals are visual, verbal and instructional signs designed to convey equality. For example, two co-teachers might take turns authoring the classroom newsletter, launch a collaborative Instagram account or host a few classroom events as a pair.

What parity signals are you sending? If you can't identify any, consider how you will communicate a united front to students, families and colleagues. Signals you might adopt include:

> » *putting both of your names on the board, the door, paperwork and classroom websites*
> » *routinely talking to your students about your shared roles as teachers*
> » *ensuring both teachers are entered into the electronic grade book as instructors*
> » *creating a hybrid name for your teaching team (à la Kimye and Bradgelina and not unlike our favorites: Jula and Paulie)*
> » *setting up the classroom to accommodate both teachers and to make collaboration easier (e.g., pushing your desks together)*
> » *wearing matching T-shirts, ties or "I love co-teaching" suspenders*
> » *creating fun rituals perfect for two people like knock-knock jokes, call and response chants (e.g., "I say 'fusion', you say 'fission'") and impromptu dance-offs (for teachers too funky for mere jokes and chants)*
> » *using words like "we" and "our" in discussing the classroom, the curriculum and students*

» *starting the day or the class period at the helm of the classroom as a team or routinely switching roles in this ritual*

» *sharing the responsibility of communicating with parents*

» *attending student conferences together*

» *attending professional development activities together*

» *eliminating labels that communicate role division (e.g., special education teacher, ELL teacher, general education teacher)*

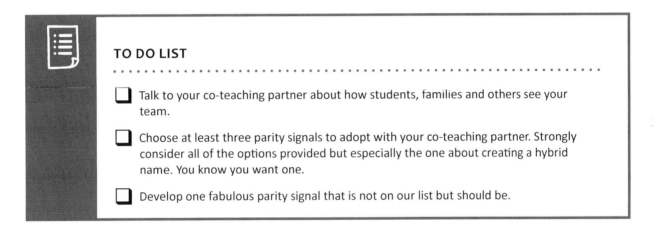

TO DO LIST

☐ Talk to your co-teaching partner about how students, families and others see your team.

☐ Choose at least three parity signals to adopt with your co-teaching partner. Strongly consider all of the options provided but especially the one about creating a hybrid name. You know you want one.

☐ Develop one fabulous parity signal that is not on our list but should be.

REVIEW ROLES
& RESPONSIBILITIES

Co-teaching ultimately should make your professional life less stressful and more fulfilling. This is, in part, because you will be able to teach more creatively and effectively, but also because you have someone with whom you can share roles and responsibilities. No longer do you have to grade those papers alone by the flickering fluorescent lights of the faculty lounge. Gone are the days of supervising twenty exploding volcanoes with just one teacher, one clipboard and one goop-crusted lab coat. Say goodbye to navigating that new IEP software with only the class frog, Hopper, sitting nearby to support your work.

On Day 11, we want you to consider new possibilities and begin to have explicit conversations about how work will be assigned in a shared classroom. In this section, we will explore roles and responsibilities in two ways. First, we will look at a tool that will help co-teaching teams discuss and delegate the various roles and responsibilities that are part of a co-taught classroom. Then, we will outline ideas for expanding roles and experimenting with new responsibilities to better serve students and to help you grow your teaching skills and competencies.

Divide & Conquer

Who will contact parents to schedule meetings related to behavior plans? Who will make sure a student has the necessary assistive technology for each lesson? Who will check assignment notebooks on Fridays? Who will direct and who will cast the upcoming production of *The Periodic Table: A Musical* in your sixth and seventh period classes? These are important conversations, and they serve as a reminder of just how much there is to do in a typical classroom.

The first step in creating an equitable division of labor in your partnership is considering all of the possible teaching roles and responsibilities that are part of a well-functioning classroom. You can make your own list or you can use Figure 11.1 to start your conversation. Working as a team, discuss the items on the list and determine who is or should be primarily responsible for each task or job. This list can be a very powerful tool for communication as it can help teams consider not only the roles and responsibilities they will delegate and adopt, but also those they would like to try for the first time and those they already share or would like to share.

Take On New Roles

Teams that are making the most out of their co-teaching arrangement understand that general educators need not be the only ones delivering lessons, special educators need not be the only ones supporting individual students and paraprofessionals need not focus their support, guidance and attention on learners with disabilities alone. To get the most out of your co-teaching relationship, you and your partner should regularly take turns trying new roles and taking on new responsibilities—even if it is only for a few minutes a day or a few hours each month. This type of role sharing helps to communicate to students that all educators teach all students. It also serves as an inexpensive and powerful staff development tool as the adults in the classroom learn skills from new challenges and experiences.

In order to achieve this level of collaboration and role sharing, co-teaching teams must take seriously the idea that no single role belongs to any one adult. In collaborative classrooms, a speech-language pathologist might teach a small reading group including students with and without identified disabilities; a special educator might work on an independent project with a student without disabilities; a general educator might work one-on-one with a student with Down syndrome; and a social worker might teach social skills to an entire second-grade class.

When you find yourselves in a slump, when you have been doing business in the same ways for weeks or even months without "mixing it up" or when you have wanted to do something differently but have not yet taken the plunge, it is especially important to consider different roles and responsibilities. It is also a signal to switch things up when you feel overworked or unchallenged. You and your partner are probably in need of a "role and responsibility review" when:

» *The general educator on your team has never has a chance to work individually with students with disabilities.*
» *The special educator on your team is not regularly planning and teaching whole-class lessons.*
» *Therapists are rarely invited to develop curriculum or teach in the classroom.*
» *The only role of the paraprofessional in your classroom is to offer direct support to a student with a disability.*
» *Students do not have leadership roles and are never asked to present lessons with each other or with their teachers.*
» *Students say, "We are really bored with how you are defining roles and responsibilities in our classroom. Can't we jazz things up around here?"*

Certainly, we do not mean to suggest that you should change every role and responsibility you have adopted when you start co-teaching. It is important, however, that the roles and responsibilities of all team members be reviewed and assessed continuously. A model that works during one semester may need revisions in subsequent terms, and a team member who takes on certain responsibilities one year may want to try new ones the next year.

TO DO LIST

. . . .

☐ Complete the "Co-Teaching Roles & Responsibilities Checklist" with your co-teacher and any other members of your teaching team.

☐ Address any roles and responsibilities that should shift in your relationship.

☐ Plan a few lessons, routines and structures that allow you to experiment with those shifts. Then, shift away!

FIGURE 11.1

Co-Teaching Roles & Responsibilities Checklist

Read through this list of roles and responsibilities in the co-taught classroom. For each item, determine which person on your team will have (p) primary responsibility; (s) secondary responsibility; (sh) shared responsibility; and/or (i) input in the decision-making.

ROLE OR RESPONSIBILITY	GENERAL EDUCATION TEACHER	SPECIAL EDUCATION TEACHER	OTHER (e.g., parapro., speech path.)
designing differentiated curriculum, instruction & assessment			
creating student-specific modifications & adaptations			
integrating student IEP objectives into daily instruction			
creating classroom materials for all (e.g., models, word wall)			
creating adapted materials for some (e.g., assignment checklists, picture schedules)			
setting up necessary assistive technology for lessons (e.g., switches, alternate keyboards)			
providing 1:1 instruction when needed			
teaching whole-class lessons			
leading small-group lessons			
monitoring student progress			
conducting assessments			
grading (e.g., homework, quizzes)			
tabulating final grades			
completing report cards			
sharing IEP data/updates with families			
communicating with families			
participating in parent-teacher conferences			
writing the IEP			
participating in IEP meetings			
consulting with related services			
providing training for paraprofessional			
providing regular feedback for paraprofessional			
organizing planning meetings			
facilitating meetings			
facilitating peer supports (e.g., educating students about supporting one another)			
managing classroom; keeping materials/space organized			

When you have finished determining roles and responsibilities, consider the following questions:

1. *Does anyone feel uncomfortable with any of the roles as outlined?*

2. *Should any of these roles and responsibilities be changed?*

3. *Will anyone need support to engage in these roles and responsibilities?*

4. *What messages does our proposed division of responsibilities send to students, parents and our colleagues?*

Adapted from: Causton, J. & Theoharis, G. (2014). *The Principal's Handbook for Leading Inclusive Schools.* Paul H. Brookes Publishing. Baltimore, MD: pp. 80-81.

DAY 12

GET IN THE HABIT

Thinking about thinking is today's focus because we believe that co-teaching is about much more than putting two teachers in a room together; it requires constant communication, reflection and problem solving. For some, this is easy. Others may need a little help in the form of acquiring helpful habits of mind.

In this section, we will outline ten helpful habits. We don't think that these are the only habits that will help teachers succeed in co-teaching relationships, but we do feel they are important. We sometimes call this list of ten "the intangibles" because they represent the good but invisible beliefs so many teachers use to grow as professionals and help their learners succeed. Taken from one of our favorite reads, *Don't Sweat the Small Stuff and It's All Small Stuff* by Richard Carlson (1997), these ideas may—at the very least—inspire a rich discussion with your colleagues. If adopted by you and your co-teaching partner, however, the habits may do even more than get you talking; we believe they have the power to transform your collaborative relationship and your daily work in the classroom.

Thank Someone Daily

This simple strategy takes only a few seconds to complete, but it may be one of the easiest ways to strengthen teams, build relationships and identify aspects of your teaming that are going well and deserve attention.

As you think of people to thank, remember that anyone can be the focus of your gratitude—a school secretary who found your missing reading glasses, a coworker who held the door open for you or your co-teaching partner for remembering to bring Styrofoam balls for your 3-D models of the human eye. Pick one worthy person or many.

How you extend gratitude is up to you. You can shout it, send a note, scrawl it on a dry erase board, give a gift or post a public message on Facebook, Twitter or Instagram. The format is not important; the message is.

As far as the "when" of giving thanks, Carlson recommends the morning hours. We certainly encourage you to provide praise anytime the mood strikes, but try not to wait until everyone is filing out of the building at day's end to express your appreciation. Gearing your attention towards gratitude when you get to school can set the mood for a positive and productive day in the classroom and beyond.

Lighten Up

Do you commonly complain about every little thing that goes wrong? Do you grouch when your co-teaching partner forgets to return your favorite stapler? Do you roll your eyes when an impromptu staff meeting is called? Do you lose your cool when your Kindergartners put books about natural disasters in the reptiles bin? When you find yourself ruminating about minor annoyances, you are likely not at your best as a teacher or as a collaborative partner. These are the times you may need to take a minute to breathe and lighten up.

Carlson suggests that we contribute to a negative state of mind when we focus on it. So, we recommend that you try not to attend to the five-hundred-page *Health Education* textbook you just dropped on your foot, but instead celebrate the fact that the book opened to a page of stretching exercises that you can immediately use to unwind during your break. In other words, instead of obsessing on the negative, look for some light in challenging and annoying situations.

Use your co-teaching partner as an ally in your "lightening up" mission. Agree to make your class-room a low-stress environment. Decide to laugh...a lot. Practice looking on the bright side and help your partner do the same.

Pick Your Battles

"Pick your battles" is advice we can apply to our collaborative relationships and our interactions with our students. Try to remember that winning is not the point in the work that we do. Certainly there will be times when you do have to "go to battle," but try to select these situations with care. You may need to defend a student if another teacher is sharing disparaging comments about him or her in the faculty lounge, but if your co-teaching partner forgets to download game show songs to complement the *Family Feud*–style review activity you have co-planned, you might want to relax, count to ten and enjoy the game sans the peppy tunes.

Talk to your co-teacher about this one. Decide separately and then together about your non-nego-tiables. Talk about which things you feel you must fight for (e.g., getting the right supports for your students) and happenings that may not necessarily indicate a call to arms (e.g., getting assigned thirty-three students when others only have thirty-one).

Realize That Stuff Happens

Life, as they say, is "one thing after another." As soon as you traverse one speed bump, you approach another. You might get five new students two weeks into the school year. Students may "boo" you and your partner's dramatic reenactment of the law of conservation of mass. You might accidentally forward a photo of you and your co-teaching partner rocking out at the KISS concert (with your face painted in Peter Criss tiger stripes) to all of your students and their families. Stuff can happen. So why get upset when it does? These bumps are a part of life and certainly part of working in a busy co-taught classroom. Accept them. Absorb them. Move on.

Be Flexible

Were you planning to have a guest speaker when an all-school assembly was called? Did you and your partner get assigned the bad/cold/small classroom this year? Were the doughnuts gone by the time you got to the lounge during your planning period? These things are annoying for sure, but they do not signal the end of the world. To be at your professional best, expect change. Plan for it. Learn to go with the flow. Jump to an alternate plan when needed. And consider keeping a secret stash of doughnuts in your desk.

In our fast-paced modern world, flexibility is one of the greatest skills anyone can cultivate. Effective teachers know that things often do not go according to the best-laid plans. They feel comfortable changing course, when needed. They can adapt. They are willing to find a new way. They realize that rigidity in the classroom and around the planning table can create significant stress in the day and throughout the year.

To be more flexible, go out of your way to embrace your colleague's ideas, especially those you may have previously resisted. If you are not thrilled about trying the practice of "flipping" in your geometry classes, but your co-teacher has her heart set on it, surprise her by embracing the idea and trying it for a few upcoming lessons.

You can also get "flexy" by seeking out novelty. With your co-teacher at your side, make a list of new things to try and integrate these ideas into your classroom practice over the course of a quarter, semester or year.

Finally, you can work on flexibility by simply becoming aware of your own resistance. The next time you want to object to an idea, consider an alternate response. Take a moment to assess if you need to stand your ground or if this is an opportunity to bend just a bit.

Let Others Be Right

Say your co-teaching partner insisted on using a new tech tool to illustrate your teaching practices during Family Math Night. In your planning session, you expressed doubts about using a new tool on a night when time was limited and you were facing an audience you didn't assemble very often. Your co-teacher, however, loves trying new things. He insists on using the new tool. That evening, the room is filled with fifty families and the technology is not working. You are both now in the position of cobbling together a thirty-minute presentation from memory. You certainly could shoot your co-teaching partner a dirty look and let the parents know that it is his fault or you could take the high road and tell families how appreciative you are to have a partner who is not thrown by such failures and keeps pushing you to try new things in the classroom.

Sometimes, being right doesn't really matter. Depending on the situation, it might be more helpful to be kind, supportive and agreeable. And consider that if you model this habit often enough, others around you may follow suit and let you be right too.

Become More Patient

The more patient you are, the more accepting you will be of what is, and the less likely you will be to futilely resist changes, challenges and barriers. If you lack patience, life can be constantly frustrating. You may be easily annoyed and irritated. If one becomes more patient, however, work becomes a bit easier and potentially more enjoyable. Further, being more patient in collaborative relationships may result in both of you having more patience in the classroom—never a bad thing!

To become more patient, it might help to focus on what makes you the most impatient and then engage in practices to potentially change your outlook or behaviors. If you get impatient during long meetings, offer to be the facilitator so you can be productive and make a contribution while conversations linger. If you are frustrated by the new electronic grade book and the time spent learning to use it, take a deep breath and recognize how much easier assessment will be once you have mastered this tool.

Avoid Snowball Thinking

The work day can spiral out of control when you are engaged in snowball thinking. Snowballing is when one negative thought leads to another and then another and then another; stress, tension and anxiety levels build and become overwhelming. For example, imagine that you and your co-teaching partner have a new student who needs support from a mobility instructor. You wake up in the middle of the night worried about how you will address the student's needs in your middle school classroom. You have not yet met with the therapist, but instead of thinking, "I'm sure he will have several ideas we can use," you start to doubt that the meeting will be helpful. Then you start to worry about meeting the needs of all of the students in the classroom. Pretty soon you are feeling overwhelmed and thinking, "I have never had a student with low vision! How can I possibly co-teach, learn new skills and help so many learners with diverse needs succeed?"

The key to tackling snowball thinking is to be aware of this type of pattern and immediately stop the storm. Catch yourself in the act of snowballing and realize, "I'm doing it again." Label and "talk back" to this negative habit as a way of staying positive and productive in interactions with learners, parents and your other collaborative partners.

Don't Interrupt

If you have been in any meetings lately, you surely have noticed the tendency of some group members to interrupt others or finish their sentences. Carlson asks us to pause and consider what this practice communicates to our colleagues. It might seem like we are dismissing or devaluing the input of a teammate. And, as he so sagely points out, it also puts us in the position of trying to be in two heads at once. When you hurry someone along, interrupt or finish his or her sentence, you have to keep track not only of your own thoughts but of those of the person you are interrupting. This tendency encourages both parties to speed up speech and thinking and may, therefore, result in a less productive and thoughtful exchange. Also consider what the impact of this practice might be on a co-teaching partnership. If you are interrupting each other in your team meetings, you may also be doing it in the classroom and inadvertently modeling it for learners.

Repeat: Everything Is Not An Emergency

Do you know someone who acts like everything is worthy of a call to 911? Most of us do. You might notice that when you are around this person, their feelings of dread are not only a downer, but also contagious. Therefore, addressing this habit is huge because when one of you goes into emergency mode, there is a possibility that the other in your dyad will follow suit.

Acting like everything is an emergency is a dangerous practice because when we turn a little thing into a tragedy, we turn life into one great big continuing crisis. When the bus is a no-show for the field trip or the health test is not modified and you feel you are about to explode, breathe deeply and remember that neither one of these situations are red-light-drop-everything problems. Stopping to reflect and put each situation in perspective is a useful practice; continued attention to this habit can help you deal more gracefully with minor annoyances and mini-disasters alike.

One way to tame this tendency is to pay attention to how often you get upset, frustrated or overwhelmed by what could be described as "small stuff." When you find yourself in such a situation, repeat aloud, "This is not an emergency." Or better yet, say it to your co-teacher so he or she can confirm the sentiment. Then breathe. Then repeat.

Imagine Everyone Is Enlightened Except You

What if you acted as if everyone you meet is here to teach you something? Perhaps the angry parent or the student who "just won't listen" is here to teach you about patience. Maybe that critical school board candidate is in your path to teach you to be more open to other opinions.

With practice, you can get yourself in the habit of approaching life in this manner and, if you do, we think that you'll find it instructive. Often, once you discover what someone is trying to teach you, it's a bit easier to let go of your frustration. For example, suppose you have a new administrator who holds a set of beliefs that are quite different from your own. Rather than feeling irritated, ask, "What is he trying to teach me?" Maybe you need to learn about listening in a more generous way. If you focused on his message instead of on your initial feelings, perhaps you would learn something that would be helpful in your work. Or maybe you feel he really needs to be educated on a viewpoint you have. He could be teaching you to be more compelling or creative or direct as you express your own views and values.

Try employing this habit as you collaborate with your co-teaching partner. You may find it is not only useful but even a tiny bit fun. As you move from being frustrated to curious, you may not only solve some problems but begin to appreciate all of the "enlightened ones" around you.

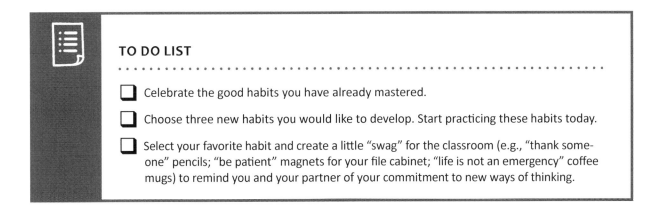

TO DO LIST

- [ ] Celebrate the good habits you have already mastered.

- [ ] Choose three new habits you would like to develop. Start practicing these habits today.

- [ ] Select your favorite habit and create a little "swag" for the classroom (e.g., "thank someone" pencils; "be patient" magnets for your file cabinet; "life is not an emergency" coffee mugs) to remind you and your partner of your commitment to new ways of thinking.

DAY 13

BUILD A COMMUNITY

Although no teacher can inspire friendships among students, every educator can create conditions in the classroom that will give them opportunities to strengthen social relationships, learn about and from each other and get and give support. The hope is, of course, that these opportunities will eventually lead to the development of friendships. Research suggests that students cannot learn effectively when they feel uncomfortable, unsafe or at-risk in some way (Chen, 2007; Ripski & Gregory, 2009), so creating an enviable classroom is critical for student comfort, and also for academic success.

Of course, creating a supportive and positive classroom culture is not a recommendation only for co-teachers; we believe every educator should be focused on this goal. The reason we are targeting this piece of advice in a book on co-teaching is because we feel that ongoing community building is easier to teach and support when two adults are prioritizing it as a goal. Further, two teachers have a lot of creative options for teaching about reciprocity, relationships and support. For instance, co-teachers can model encouragement for one another in front of students or demonstrate a bit of innocent teasing by engaging in an ongoing practical joke (e.g., planting a whoopee cushion on one another's chairs). Teachers flying solo can do these things with their students' support, of course, but co-teachers get to try these tricks with both students and another adult. Possibilities are, therefore, amplified!

We have two big ideas to share on Day 13. For starters, we will give you some quick strategies for building a community. Then, we will introduce you to a handful of community-building games you can use to bring learners together and teach them how to listen to and learn from one another.

Community-Building Strategies

There are many ways to engage in the work of community building. You can involve students in conversations about the topic, select materials to emphasize or reinforce messages of connection and support and emphasize practices that build social skills. The five ideas outlined in this section will help you achieve these goals. Try one or all of these to bring a sense of safety and shared purpose into your learning space.

Clear Expression Of Values

Talk to your students about the beliefs and values of the classroom and set some guidelines related to those values. You might call this a mission statement or a philosophy. In one middle school classroom we visited, the following beliefs were elicited from teachers and students and were posted on the wall:

> » **We are all learners and we are all teachers.** *We will create opportunities in this classroom to share expertise and to take on new roles in both teaching and learning.*
> » **Difference is normal and expected.** *We will not all work at the same rate, have the same preferences, work best with the same classmates or need the same things to succeed.*
> » **Support should be reciprocal.** *We are all expected to give support to and get support from one another.*
> » **Uniqueness is encouraged.** *We should all feel free to express ourselves. We should not be afraid to take risks, ask questions or march to the beat of a different drummer in this classroom.*
> » **Fair does not mean equal.** *We may not get "the same" as our classmates when it comes to classroom materials, choices, personal supports/cues and so on. We are individuals, and we will be treated like the unique individuals we are.*

What are the expectations, beliefs or values evident in your classroom? Can you find a way of expressing them to students or creating them with your learners?

Appreciations

Appreciations can come in many forms. One way to introduce the idea of gratitude is to create a game. For instance, you might choose a different student each week to sit in the "sweet spot," a chair positioned at the front of the classroom. The student in this seat gets to spend a few minutes receiving thanks and compliments from classmates. Appreciations can also be woven into curriculum and instruction. Have students practice writing a formal letter by thanking a fellow student, a former teacher or a community member. Or you can work on verbal communication skills by occasionally having students give short orange juice toasts to one another.

Keep in mind that appreciations should not be seen as a tool to use only with the little ones. We have been delighted to see compliment-centered Twitter accounts popping up at high schools around the country. Messages we have read include, "@MegS— helped me in math today in a BIG way. Thx girl" and "Ryan K & @P— : nicest guys - thx for fixing my car!"

Humor

You and your co-teaching partner don't need backgrounds in comedy in order to lighten the classroom mood and strengthen the community. Use humorous anecdotes, jokes, entertaining video clips, cartoons, silly visuals (e.g., stand on a real soap box when you get on your "soap box") and drama to bring laughter and levity into daily work.

Class Meetings

Have class meetings all year long. Use them to vote on issues, solve problems, discuss concerns and plan special trips or events. Students learn to become active members in a community when they get to participate in building it, determine rules and guidelines for it and deal with challenges that arise with the members of that group.

Read Alouds

Create a community where conversations about differences are commonplace and where students can not only ask and answer questions, but build on their knowledge and understanding throughout the year. One way to expand the experiences and perspectives of all students is to share books about human differences as part of a whole-class read aloud. Books might be selected with any number of themes in mind including teaming, collaboration, diversity, differences, community, disability, support, friendship, character and social change. See Table 13.1 for titles that will help your students explore these topics.

If this recommendation is not possible due to the subject area or grade level you teach, you might share news items or short articles instead. If you are a science teacher, for instance, you could discuss a magazine piece about Temple Grandin's expertise in animal science and include information about autism. If you are a math teacher, the story of Alan Turing and his gifts of code breaking could be shared alongside a conversation about his sexual orientation and subsequent punishment for it. This could be paired with a brief conversation about how to make the classroom safe for everyone regardless of differences in sexuality or gender expression.

Community-Building Games

A variety of community-building games, such as those featured in this section, can be used to enhance relationships in the classroom, encourage friendships and foster student-to-student learning opportunities. Although all of these activities can be used at the beginning of the year to help students become familiar with one another, they should not be abandoned thereafter. Use them in September and look for opportunities to integrate them into your lessons throughout the year.

Back-To-Back

This game focuses on celebrating commonalities. It can help students understand that they are more alike than different, and it can provide them with starting points for making new connections with classmates.

To play, have students sit or stand back to back. Ask them to talk over their shoulders to each other and come up with things they have in common. For example, "I have a younger brother," or "I love hockey." If any statement is true for both of the partners, they turn around, jump into the air and give each other a high-five.

This activity can be a getting-to-know-you game, or it can be used in the context of daily lessons. Students might share things they have in common about their families (before a Kindergarten unit on that topic) or things they have in common related to reading preferences and habits (before a conversation about genres).

Race To Write

Race to Write is meant to encourage brainstorming, collaboration and sharing. It should help students see that each member of a group brings a different collection of ideas, experiences and expertise to the table.

To play, divide students into teams of four and give each team several sheets of chart paper. Then, set a timer and have the students scribble answers to prompts that are related to community building, such as ideas for creating a safe classroom space or random acts of kindness. At the end of a set period of time, have students share their answers. The products that students create can be shared verbally, posted on a classroom blog or pinned up on a bulletin board.

Like Back-to-Back, this activity can be used to review standards-based content. Instead of asking learners to brainstorm about the community, however, you can have them record examples of hyperbole, things that people estimate or characteristics of a democracy.

Line Up

The purpose of this next community builder is to help students see that while people in a group may have very different beliefs and values, they can still listen to and potentially learn from one another. Remind students of this goal before you play and also when you conclude the activity.

To begin, place signs on one wall of your classroom to create a visual continuum (e.g., never/ sometimes/almost always/always). Then, read prompts or sentences aloud (e.g., "I intervene when I see someone being bullied"; "I draw for fun") and ask students to find a spot in line as a way to respond. For example, if you announce, "I do my best during group work," and a student feels this is a strength for him, he would move near the "always" sign. After all learners have found a spot on the line, have them turn and talk to a partner standing nearby about why they made the choice they did. Or have students "fold" their line in half and discuss the given prompt with the partner standing across from them. In this formation, students who responded "always" will most likely be paired with students who responded "never." This pairing of opposites then becomes an opportunity to teach skills such as active listening and perspective taking.

Want to convert this community builder to an energizer, informal assessment or review game? Just align your questions with lesson-related topics. For example, after reading *Charlotte's Web*, students might answer, "I think animals communicate with each other," or "I think kids sometimes understand animals better than adults do."

What's In My Pocket?

This activity is designed to help students share something personal without having to rely too much on spoken words. It often prompts funny or particularly poignant moments as students reflect on why and how we use objects to remember, support and inspire.

Get started by asking students to find something in their desks or lockers that has meaning to them. This might be a necklace, an eraser, their lunch box, a photo from their wallet or a keychain. When all students have located something, have them find partners or get into small groups and share their items with one another. Prompt students to ask questions like, "What makes this object meaningful to you?" and "Why did you select it?" Cue partners to focus on listening.

When all students have finished sharing, bring the large group back together to debrief. You might ask what students learned from one another or what similarities and differences they noticed as objects and stories were shared.

To use this idea in daily lessons, ask students to bring in objects that certain historical or literary figures might have in their pockets. For instance, students might bring in pencils, memo pads and coins from around the world when they are learning about Nelly Bly.

Five-Minute Interview

This quick and easy community builder provides opportunities for students to "dive deeper" to learn about their classmates. It also focuses on asking and answering questions so it can help learners practice communication skills such as paraphrasing, turn-taking, staying on topic and seeking clarification.

The first step of this game is to invite students to write down a list of potential interview questions. If you teach younger children or have learners who would struggle with this task, you can instead provide a list of possible questions and let them choose the ones they want to ask. Here are a few we like to use across age groups:

> » *What is your most treasured memory with a parent or grandparent?*
> » *What would be your ideal vacation?*
> » *What is your favorite book?*
> » *Do you have a collection? If so, what do you collect?*
> » *Would you rather go fishing, go shopping or "just pass GO" in Monopoly?*
> » *If you could invent a flavor of ice cream, what would be in it?*
> » *Are you more of a dog person, a cat person, a fish person or a person person?*
> » *If you could live inside any television show, which one would you pick?*
> » *What one item would you bring with you to a deserted island?*
> » *What do you like most about physical education class/art class/music class?*
> » *What is your favorite kind of music? Favorite song?*
> » *Have you helped someone this week? If so, what did you do to be helpful?*

Then, assign each student a partner and instruct the pair to begin their interviews. For five minutes one student is the interviewer and the other is the interviewee. Make it clear that the interviewee is free to pass on any questions that he or she cannot or does not want to answer. After the five minutes elapse, have students switch roles. Following this exercise, have students discuss what they learned about their partners, what surprised them about the discussion, what questions they felt were the best and the toughest and so on.

Want to change this one up and use it for content introduction or review? Simply use questions that are connected to your subject matter but also allow students to learn from a peer. Questions to introduce a unit on nutrition might be:

» *To you, what does healthy eating mean?*
» *What is your healthiest eating habit?*
» *What is your worst eating habit?*
» *What is a healthy dish you know how to prepare?*
» *In your opinion, what can schools do to help students make healthier food choices?*

IMPLEMENTATION TIP

Assign a student to select and facilitate a community builder each day or at least each week. One teacher we know keeps descriptions of 184 activities in a recipe box that sits atop her desk. Adults and students in the classroom take turns choosing, planning and leading the activities.

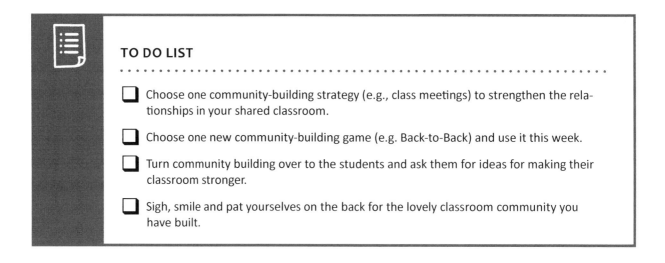

TO DO LIST

☐ Choose one community-building strategy (e.g., class meetings) to strengthen the relationships in your shared classroom.

☐ Choose one new community-building game (e.g. Back-to-Back) and use it this week.

☐ Turn community building over to the students and ask them for ideas for making their classroom stronger.

☐ Sigh, smile and pat yourselves on the back for the lovely classroom community you have built.

TABLE 13.1
Read Aloud Suggestions

Chapter books about differences, community and support

Alexie, Sherman.
The Absolutely True Diary of a Part-Time Indian.
New York: Little, Brown & Company, 2009

Buyea, Rob.
Because of Mr. Terupt.
New York: Yearling, 2011.

Choldenko, Gennifer.
Al Capone Does My Shirts.
New York: Penguin, 2006.

Cisneros, Sandra.
The House on Mango Street.
New York: Vintage, 1984.

Clements, Andrew.
About Average.
New York: Atheneum, 2014.

Creech, Sharon.
The Boy on the Porch.
New York: HarperCollins, 2013.

Draper, Sharon.
Out of My Mind.
New York: Atheneum, 2010.

Fleischman, Paul.
Seedfolks.
New York: HarperCollins, 1997.

Hall, Kenneth.
Asperger Syndrome, the Universe and Everything.
London, PA: Jessica Kingsley, 2001.

Hyde, Catherine Ryan.
Pay It Forward: Young Readers Edition.
New York: Simon & Schuster, 2014.

Jackson, Luke.
Freaks, Geeks, and Asperger Syndrome: A User Guide to Adolescence.
London, PA: Jessica Kingsley, 2002.

Lean, Sarah.
A Dog Called Homeless.
New York: Katherine Tegen Books, 2014.

Lombard, Jenny.
Drita, My Homegirl.
New York: Puffin, 2008.

Lord, Cynthia
Rules.
New York: Scholastic, 2013.

Howe, James.
The Misfits.
New York: Atheneum, 2003.

Mass, Wendy.
A Mango-Shaped Space.
New York: Little, Brown & Company, 2003.

Palacio, R. J.
Wonder.
New York: Alfred A. Knopf, 2012.

Philbrick, Rodman.
Freak the Mighty.
New York: Scholastic, 1993.

Spinelli, Jerry.
Loser.
New York: HarperCollins, 2003.

Van Draanen, Wendelin.
The Running Dream.
New York: Random House, 2011.

Woodson, Jacqueline.
Feathers.
New York: Penguin, 2009.

Picture books about differences, community and support

Asare, Meshack.
Sosu's Call.
La Jolla, CA: Kane/Miller Book Publishers, 2002.

Beaumont, Karen.
I Like Myself.
New York: Houghton Mifflin Harcourt, 2010.

Caseley, Judith.
Harry and Willy and Carrothead.
New York: Greenwillow Books, 1991.

Elliot, Rebecca.
Just Because.
Oxford: Lion Hudson PLC, 2011.

Kraus, Robert.
Leo the Late Bloomer.
New York: HarperCollins, 1994.

Leonni, Leo.
Swimmy.
New York: Dragonfly Books, 1971.

Most, Bernard.
The Cow That Went OINK.
New York: Voyager Books, 2003.

Nazareth Elementary School.
Our Friend Mikayla.
Raleigh, NC: The Bubel/Aiken Foundation, 2006.

Parr, Todd.
It's Okay to Be Different.
Boston, MA: Little, Brown Books for Young Readers, 2011.

Polacco, Patricia.
Mr. Lincoln's Way.
New York: Philomel Books, 2001.

Rabinowitz, Alan.
A Boy and a Jaguar.
New York: Houghton Mifflin Harcourt, 2014.

DAY 14

"SHAKE UP" YOUR STRUCTURES

If an observer walks into your classroom day after day, week after week, what would he or she see:

a) *two teachers at the helm*

b) *one teacher at the helm and one sitting or standing in the back of the room*

c) *one teacher at the helm and one "floating" through the room to check in with other students*

d) *a combination of a, b and c*

e) *both teachers cowering in the back of the room, overwhelmed and unsure of which collaborative structure to use*

f) *a wide range of collaborative structures and different arrangements of staff, students, desks and materials*

If you answered (f) to this question, you can skip this section and the next few as well because you are far ahead of the curve when it comes to getting the most from your human resources, collaborating effectively and using a co-teaching model to differentiate instruction.

If you answered (e), however, we are so glad you are reading this book. We are here to help.

So now that we have covered two ends of the spectrum, we are guessing that the rest of you answered a, b, c or d. If you did, you are not alone. Many co-teaching teams are either unsure of how to expand the range of collaborative structures they use or feel they do not have the time or resources to try something new.

On Day 14, we want to provide you with the support you may be seeking. In these next few pages, we hope to convince you that new structures do not necessarily take more time to implement and that "shaking them up" regularly can not only help you support students more effectively, but also invigorate your teaching. We will start with the basics by introducing you to what we call the core collaborative structures: duet teaching, one teach/one assist, one teach/one float and one teach/ one make multisensory.

Duet Teaching

Duet teaching is one of the most common teaching structures and needs to be mastered before you move on to any other model. Why? Because duet teaching requires both educators in a co-teaching partnership to demonstrate their equal status to learners and to work together directly. Duet teaching (Greene & Isaacs, 1999) involves two adults working together to provide instruction. A "duet" lesson or lesson segment typically involves both adults engaging in primary teaching roles in the class; instructors collaboratively lead class discussions, answer student questions or facilitate lectures and activities.

Students need to see their teachers working and teaching together, so the duet structure should be used regularly. However, it cannot and should not be the primary model you use day in and day out. If your school has combined students and resources to make co-teaching a reality, this has happened so that learners can profit not only from the expertise of two people, but from all of the different ways that classrooms can behave, look and feel when there is more than one adult available to provide supports and deliver instruction. If your administrators have increased the number of students in each classroom due to co-teaching (which they likely have) and brought students with and without disabilities together to learn in a resource-rich setting, you have a responsibility to teach and plan "out of the box." If a team co-teaches primarily using a duet model, they are not making the most out of having two adults in the classroom and students are getting an experience that is not much different from the one they could have had with just one teacher and fewer classmates.

Having shared that caution, we do feel that duet teaching is critical to the success of a co-taught classroom. Using it on a regular basis communicates to students that their teachers are equals. It demonstrates that you and your partner know how to build off of the expertise and skills of one another, not only behind the scenes but in front of your most important audience: your students. Mastering duet teaching will undoubtedly help you communicate better with your partner and flesh out your strengths and weaknesses as individuals and as a teaching team.

It may be helpful to use duet teaching to:

» *introduce a unit or lesson*
» *conclude a unit or lesson*
» *facilitate a class meeting*
» *play a whole-class game*
» *engage in a community-building exercise*

One Teach/One Assist

In the one teach/one assist model, educators typically share lesson delivery responsibilities; one leads the lesson while the other supports in some way (Cook and Friend, 1995). The lead person is usually in charge of the content while the assisting teacher adds examples, distributes supplies or checks in with students.

When many educators start co-teaching, it is the one teach/one assist model that they may initially find the most comfortable. Any teacher who has tried to write while talking or distribute materials without losing his or her train of thought will appreciate having another set of hands in the room to make lessons stronger and more seamless and is, therefore, likely to fall immediately in like with one teach/one assist. We have had our own moments of enchantment with one teach/one assist and agree that this structure should be used regularly in a co-taught classroom.

Like duet teaching, however, teams must take care not to overdo the use of one teach/one assist. According to a 2007 study by Scruggs, Mastropieri and McDuffie, this model is often significantly overused in co-taught classrooms. Some teams fall into a pattern where the general education teacher leads and the special education teacher assists for all or nearly all lessons. When this happens, students do not see their teachers working as a team and educators do not have many opportunities to acquire new collaborative skills as they teach together each day. Therefore, when you are using one teach/one assist, be sure to vary who takes the lead. Both teachers should regularly lead and both teachers should regularly assist.

Think also about how you are using one teach/one assist. That is, be sure that both of you are contributing to the lesson in a meaningful way. If, for example, you have noticed that when you use this structure, one teacher morphs from assistant teacher mode into parrot mode (providing assistance by simply repeating the directions, statements and questions posed by his or her partner), you may want to rethink how you are implementing one teach/one assist. Be sure that both of your roles add to the lesson and be sure parroting is left to the birds.

It may be helpful to use one teach/one assist to:

> » *set up a complex presentation or demonstration*
> » *manage a lesson with new learning tools or assistive technology*
> » *manage a lesson with a lot of directions or transitions*
> » *set up the classroom for a change in activities*
> » *connect with individual students needing clarification or support*

One Teach/One Float

One teach/one float is another common co-teaching structure. On occasion, it is the most appropriate way to use human resources. One teach/one float is a perfect model to use, for instance, during lessons where one teacher is demonstrating something that students need to imitate. So, if one teacher is showing learners how to create land forms with modeling clay, the second teacher can be floating from desk to desk to give support and critique on the sculptures. Or during a lesson that introduces graphing calculators, one teacher may be providing the primary instruction while the other moves around the room to see if students have questions about the work assigned or the use of the calculators themselves.

Like duet teaching and one teach/one assist, one teach/one float is often a bit too familiar to students in co-taught classrooms. One teach/one float should be used sparingly, particularly if it has taken the form of one teacher leading whole-class instruction, while the other crouches next to students' desks and whispers to them in between lecture points. If you are the floater in this scenario, you are probably not only frustrated by how the structure is being implemented, but also by the knee burns you have undoubtedly acquired.

This is not to suggest that one teach/one float is always ineffective or that it is always abused by those who use it regularly. It should be noted, however, that there are many co-teaching structures that should be used across the weeks and months of the school year and one teach/one float is but one of them. If you are using one teach/one float, you are probably engaged in whole-class instruction. In co-taught classrooms, whole-class instruction should be used sparingly; therefore, one teach/one float should also be used sparingly.

It may be helpful to use one teach/one float to:

» *get students started on independent work or group work*
» *help students assemble into any assigned pairings or groupings*
» *ensure that students are following along with a demonstration, model or example*
» *ensure that students are participating/understanding directions/aware of expected behaviors*
» *provide assistance with any materials or adaptive equipment students are accessing (e.g., specialized seating, standers, slant boards)*

One Teach/One Make Multisensory

This co-teaching structure is one of our favorites because it is so flexible; there are surely hundreds of ways to create a one teach/one make multisensory lesson. In this structure, teachers think beyond how to work together and focus on how to teach creatively. To reach this goal, teaching teams may integrate any number of strategies and tools into their lessons, including but not limited to dramatic reenactments, costumes and props, audio cues or music, visuals, presentation software, apps and websites.

One teach/one make multisensory appeals to us as inclusive schooling enthusiasts because it is such a great tool for differentiating instruction for the diverse learners in your classroom. As a way to make this point, we like to ask teachers in our workshops to take any lesson that they would typically teach alone and morph it into a one teach/one make multisensory model. Through this exercise, educators see that any lesson can be "punched up" with an additional mode of output and that two teachers who are multisensory-minded can do more than just bring two perspectives into a classroom—they can dramatically expand a lesson's reach and impact.

This is not to say that we feel one teach/one make multisensory is the best possible co-teaching model. In fact, it too can become stale from overuse, but if you vary how you use it on a regular basis, this model can give your lessons a lot of "oomph" and can provide you with options for appealing to students with a very wide range of learning styles.

It may be helpful to use one teach/one make multisensory to:

> » *offer more than one mode of output during a lesson (e.g., auditory and visual)*
> » *add interest, humor or a bit of drama to a lesson*
> » *show off a new tech tool*
> » *engage in a demonstration*
> » *provide a memorable introduction or conclusion to a unit of study*

Because we feel this model has so much potential for supporting and teaching all students, we are including a list of twenty ideas for using one teach/one make multisensory in your classroom in Table 14.1.

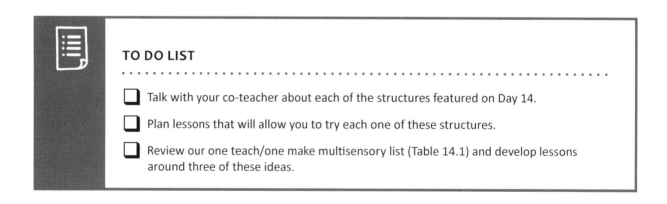

TO DO LIST

☐ Talk with your co-teacher about each of the structures featured on Day 14.

☐ Plan lessons that will allow you to try each one of these structures.

☐ Review our one teach/one make multisensory list (Table 14.1) and develop lessons around three of these ideas.

TABLE 14.1

20 Ideas for One Teach/One Make Multisensory Lessons

WHILE ONE TEACHER...	THE OTHER...
reads a passage from a book	dramatically acts out the scene
reads a passage from a book	maps the story on chart paper
reads a passage from a book	follows along with a one-person puppet show
tells/reads a story	adds in special effects (e.g., dims lights, rattles blinds and stomps feet)
conducts a mini-lecture	demonstrates how to take notes on the interactive whiteboard
conducts a mini-lecture	holds up props/objects to make key concepts memorable
conducts a mini-lecture	holds up pictures or projects images to make key concepts memorable
conducts a mini-lecture	demonstrates the use of a new augmentative communication device (e.g., uses a single-message "talker" to echo important phrases)
conducts a mini-lecture	leads a chant to emphasize targeted words/concepts
conducts a whole-class discussion	illustrates using sketchnoting
conducts a whole-class discussion	models how to complete a related graphic organizer (e.g., story map, flowchart)
conducts a whole-class discussion	adds in relevant signs or gestures (especially helpful if a student in the classroom is using or learning American Sign Language)
conducts a whole-class discussion	leads class in a movement or action related to the topic (e.g., students stand and position arms to represent obtuse, acute and right angles during a geometry lesson)
conducts a whole-class discussion	runs around the classroom (possibly in a plaid game-show-host-style jacket) getting various students to stand and make contributions, provide a physical response or shout out answers
explains an upcoming lab, project or activity	physically demonstrates the steps of the lab, project or activity
explains an upcoming lab, project or activity	plays video clips or holds up big cue cards to illustrate each step of the lab, project or activity
introduces a new concept	adds in music clips to make the lesson richer (e.g., plays "God Save the King", "Yankee Doodle" and "The Rebels" during a lesson on Lexington and Concord)
introduces a new concept	adds in audio cues to make important points memorable (e.g., plays parts of famous speeches as rhetoric is discussed)
introduces a new concept	makes the experience 4-D with props (e.g., adds "rain" to a discussion of the water cycle by misting students with a spray bottle)
introduces a new concept	demonstrates a piece of assistive technology (e.g., talking calculator, switch)

PARALLEL PERFECTLY

There are so many benefits to co-teaching, but one of the most celebrated is the ability that teachers have to decrease the student-to-teacher ratio and provide a more personalized education to every learner in the classroom. One co-teaching model that instantly creates these opportunities is parallel teaching. Read on as we explore the "what," the "why" and the "where the heck" of this powerful co-teaching structure.

The "What" Of Parallel Teaching

Parallel teaching (Cook & Friend, 1995) usually involves splitting the class into two sections. In this model, each teacher is responsible for one of these groups. This structure is useful when students "need opportunities to respond aloud, to engage in hands-on activities, or to interact with one another" (Cook & Friend, 1995, p. 7). In other words, parallel teaching should be used when a more intimate learning situation is desired.

Parallel teaching is often used to deliver the same exact content to two groups, but it can also be used when teachers want to introduce students to two different activities, concepts or ideas. In this version, the two instructors split the group, teach different content for some part of the class and then switch groups and repeat the lesson with the other half of the class, or don't switch and let students return to the larger group and share the new content with their peers. For example, a fifth-grade class might split into two groups of equal size, with one group learning about the US Congress from one teacher and the other group focusing on the US Senate. The students could then come back into a whole-class format and teach the content to one other by creating Venn diagrams, or by pairing off to share the content learned in their respective groups.

And there are still other ways to engineer parallel teaching. You can split students into two groups based on their interests and conduct a series of mini-lessons in this formation. Or you can separate students into uneven clusters if you want one teacher to be able to work with a much smaller group from time to time. Interested in even more ideas? Check out Table 15.1 for a list of twenty ways you can use parallel teaching in the co-taught classroom.

The "Why" Of Parallel Teaching

There are many benefits to using parallel teaching in the co-taught classroom. First of all, educators have opportunities to communicate that they have equal roles in the classroom; both are teaching and, in many cases, both are teaching the same content in the same way. Another benefit is being able to connect more directly and informally with students. It can be difficult—even with two teachers—to make connections with individuals in a classroom of thirty or more students. It is much easier to get to know learners and provide appropriate feedback in a group that is half that size. Finally, many students relish the opportunity to work in a small group. These learners may be more willing or able to share comments and contribute to discussions when they do not have to speak up in an entire roomful of their classmates.

The "Where The Heck Is It" Of Parallel Teaching

So, with all of the promise of parallel teaching, why don't we see more of it in co-taught classrooms? There are actually many reasons educators are lukewarm on this model. Some see it as inappropriate for teams with an uneven knowledge base. Others don't feel they have the space to parallel easily. Still others may think it is ineffective; they may question splitting the group to teach something twice that can be taught "just as easily" in a whole-group situation. We feel that parallel teaching is too powerful of a structure to be ignored because of some of its perceived problems, so we have provided responses to some common objections in Table 15.2. We encourage co-teaching teams to review this table and consider how to tackle any barriers that may arise in the planning and implementation of parallel teaching. And then, we invite you to start planning your first parallel lesson. Sure, you will miss your co-teaching pal in those moments you are working in separate spaces or in opposite corners of the classroom, but if absence does make the heart grow fonder, this model may not only help you differentiate instruction, but it could also bring you and your partner closer together. Awwwww.

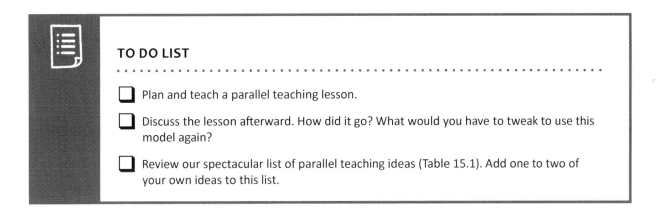

TO DO LIST

- ☐ Plan and teach a parallel teaching lesson.
- ☐ Discuss the lesson afterward. How did it go? What would you have to tweak to use this model again?
- ☐ Review our spectacular list of parallel teaching ideas (Table 15.1). Add one to two of your own ideas to this list.

TABLE 15.1

20 Ideas for Parallel Teaching Lessons

1. Two teachers teach the same content.

2. Two teachers teach the same content using different materials (e.g., one group uses assistive technology to accommodate students with disabilities).

3. Two teachers assess students using the same tools or instruments.

4. Two teachers assess students using two different tools or instruments (based on student needs and abilities).

5. Two teachers assess students using two different tools or instruments; groups then switch so that both groups are assessed in two different ways.

6. Two teachers teach different but related content (e.g., mitosis/meiosis; Axis Powers/Allied Forces; circle graphs/bar graphs); groups then switch.

7. Two teachers teach different but related content; students then pair up to teach the new material to one another.

8. Two teachers teach different but related content, groups then come back together and engage in a whole-class discussion.

9. Two teachers lead a discussion on the same topic.

10. Two teachers lead discussions on different but related topics; groups then switch.

11. Two teachers lead discussions on different but related topics; groups then come back together and engage in a whole-class discussion.

12. One teacher teaches a lesson and the other lets students explore hands-on materials, artifacts or manipulatives that may be in limited supply (e.g., rocks and minerals); groups then switch.

13. One teacher teaches a lesson and the other lets students access technology tools that may be in limited supply (e.g., tablets, heart monitors, microscopes); groups then switch.

14. One teacher teaches a lesson and the other teacher creates a product with students (e.g., mini-movie, screenplay, sculpture, DNA model); groups then switch.

15. One teacher teaches a lesson and the other conducts a review session; groups then switch.

16. One teacher teaches a lesson and the other engages in a demonstration; groups then switch.

17. One teacher teaches a lesson and the other conducts a formal or informal assessment (e.g., focus group); groups then switch.

18. One teacher teaches a lesson and the other takes students on an in-school "field trip" (e.g., library, school garden); groups then switch.

19. Two teachers conduct the same experiment, demonstration or skit.

20. Two teachers conduct related experiments, demonstrations or skits; groups then switch.

TABLE 15.2

Wise & Well-Crafted Responses to Parallel Teaching Objections

Objections to parallel teaching	Wise and well-crafted responses to parallel teaching objections
"We don't have enough room for two teachers to conduct two different lessons in my room."	Many teachers use a parallel model inside the classroom, but this is not necessarily the way you need to engineer your parallel teaching model. You might use a parallel teaching model when you have another classroom space available, when you can go outside, when the library or computer lab is open or when the lesson is conducive to working in the hallway. Having shared that, some teams find that teaching two groups in the same classroom can work effectively if simple guidelines are followed. For instance, share rules about voice volume and adapt seating so learners can sit in close proximity to one another. Young children can sit on the floor and older students can abandon desks and pull up chairs.
"My co-teacher doesn't know the material well enough to teach a lesson on it."	Teachers using a parallel teaching model do not need to be equal experts on the targeted content. Sometimes one educator may be willing to increase his or her knowledge base to teach the material. If there is a significant gap between the expertise levels of the team members, however, simply use parallel teaching to engage students differently in the two groups. One half of the class might be working on review problems with a partner while the other group learns a new concept. After an agreed-upon time period, students switch groups. In this version of parallel teaching, the teacher facilitating the review need not have the same level of content expertise as the one teaching the new material.
"Pacing is a problem. We struggle to finish our lessons at the same time. Therefore, when we come back together, groups may not have received the same content."	This is a fixable problem. It does take some practice to learn to time lessons with your co-teaching partner, but those who do acquire this skill so often find that it helps them to improve their teaching. Teams who pace their lessons together must learn to stick to their plans, manage their time and be very concise about their goals and expected outcomes. Use tools such as timers, detailed lesson plans and cell phones/texting to keep your plans in sync as much as possible. You can also teach students to begin another activity (e.g., flashcard practice, journaling) while they wait for the other half of the class to return and be ready for the next part of the lesson.
"It is disruptive to move students and desks. We lose valuable instructional time during the transitions."	This is a reasonable objection, but should not be a reason to throw parallel teaching "out with the bath water." Instead, work with students on more seamless transitions. Tighten up the process by presenting clear directions, demonstrating how you want students to move their materials and/or transition to new spaces and starting and ending lesson segments on time. Or make it into a game; use a timer and see how fast students can transition and challenge them to beat their previous transition times.
"It's easier to teach one whole-class lesson than to divide the students and teach the same content twice."	It may indeed be easier to teach whole-group lessons, but the question should not be, "Which model is easier?" The question should be, "Which model is best for students?" The answer, of course, is "all of them," meaning that teachers in the best co-taught classrooms use a wide range of structures including parallel teaching. The reason teachers should be tapping into parallel teaching—at least occasionally—is because it offers some benefits that the others do not.

TAKE YOUR STATIONS

What an embarrassment of riches! You are now familiar with five different co-teaching structures and have a range of lesson planning options for your co-taught classroom. You'd think we would be satisfied providing you with such a wealth of ideas, but we like to take things to the extreme and are, therefore, adding one more powerful structure to the mix: station teaching.

In station teaching, teachers "divide instructional content into two, three or more segments and present the content at separate locations within the classroom" (Cook & Friend, 1995, p. 6). These stations do not need to be activity-based or even teacher-led, but they often are. Similarly, two or more adults are not needed to effectively run a station teaching lesson, but this model is ideal for using the skills and expertise of two or more educators.

Setting Up Your Stations

Designing new stations is actually a very helpful exercise for teachers as it requires an understanding and a clarification of what is important for students "to know and be able to do." It's easy to generate interesting activities for stations, but it takes a bit more work to create learning experiences that target important skills and competencies and allow students to learn in varied ways.

To get started, look at your lesson objectives to determine which tasks, activities and exercises will be most appropriate to assign to individual stations. Depending on what you are teaching, you may want to provide students with opportunities for skills practice, discussion, problem solving, review of new material, partner reading, product creation or tech tool exploration. These are not the only possibilities, of course, but the structure makes any of these choices easy to implement. See Table 16.1 for an even longer list of station teaching activity ideas.

TABLE 16.1
Station Teaching Mini-Lesson/Activity Ideas

Students at stations could be asked to:

- » write poems, letters or short responses
- » develop a collaborative PowerPoint presentation with all visitors to that station
- » create a blog entry
- » design a card or board game
- » generate charts, graphs or diagrams
- » write a jingle or song
- » write a script and act out a scene
- » compile a booklet or pamphlet
- » generate a petition or survey
- » design a simulation or role play
- » compile a newspaper or newsletter
- » create a model or diorama
- » develop a set of guided notes

- » make a sketch, collage, painting, cartoon or drawing
- » audio record a speech, conversation or interview
- » create a video commercial related to content
- » shoot an e-tutorial (teach a skill or solve a problem on video)
- » complete a worksheet or problems in a textbook
- » collaboratively solve a problem
- » create a test or quiz for a segment of content
- » write a news report/bulletin
- » create an advertisement, PSA or poster
- » watch a video clip on an educational website (e.g., www. nationalgeographic.com/ video/)

- » participate in a teacher-led mini-lesson
- » participate in a student-led mini-lesson
- » engage in a small-group discussion
- » brainstorm a list of ideas or solutions
- » collect data/interpret data
- » analyze documents or artifacts
- » listen to a piece of music
- » play or compose a piece of music
- » snap and edit photos
- » create a learning station
- » facilitate an activity, game or group discussion

IMPLEMENTATION TIP

· ·

When you start using stations, use the same types of activities every time you use the structure to make planning easier. For example, a math team might consistently have a work-with-the-teacher station, an app practice station, a video "watch and learn" station and a peer review station.

The next step is to decide how many stations you will set up for a given lesson. Do you have several skills that you want students to address in a short period of time? If so, you might set up five or six stations that students will visit for just ten minutes apiece. This might be appropriate when you want to acquaint students with new materials or have them engage in drill and practice exercises. Conversely, if you need students to dive a little deeper into learning and want to carve out more time for them to work, you might create just three stations that they access for twenty minutes at a time. There is no amount of time that is necessarily best for station teaching rotations. Instead, the amount of time that students spend at each station should be determined by the objectives of your lesson and the needs of your students.

Finally, consider how you will direct the flow and assignment of your stations. You can allow students to choose stations, to repeat stations or to work on stations one at a time with every learner starting at Station #1 and advancing only when they complete the assigned task there. The most common type of station teaching lesson, however, involves the creation of a handful of stations that all students visit at some point during the lesson. A group of students begins working at each station and when a cue is given, all of them rotate. If the stations are numbered, students move in order (e.g., those at Station #4 move to Station #5; those at Station #5 move to Station #1).

See Table 16.2 for examples of several station teaching lessons.

Conducting A Station Teaching Lesson

When you design a station teaching lesson for the first time, there are a few issues of logistics to address. As with parallel teaching, some teaching teams we have coached have given up on station teaching almost as soon as they started due to problems with implementation. Therefore, we have provided a snazzy compilation of common objections to station teaching and wise and well-crafted responses to those objections (see Table 16.3). Although we do agree that the logistics involved in this model can be challenging at times, station teaching is so unique and effective for diverse groups of students, we believe it is well worth the effort.

If you are one of those seeing more challenges than benefits in this model, remember that a little planning goes a long way. We suspect that if you spend a bit of time setting up your work space, deciding on a process for transitions and creating necessary learning materials, you will quickly see the advantages of using this dynamic model. It might even become your favorite way to collaborate!

Work Space

Plan your work space. If students will be engaged in an activity that does not require a lot of materials, such as a group discussion or work on one-to-one devices, it may be best to shove desks aside and create stations from clusters of chairs. In other cases, it may work best to use classroom tables or to assemble desks into work stations by pushing a few of them together.

Each station should be marked with a sign that outlines the task directions. Provide directions that are short and simple but clear. Keep in mind that you may need to add illustrated or audio directions for young children or learners with disabilities. One team we coached used recordable birthday cards for this purpose. They covered them with paper, wrote the directions for each station on the front of the card and used the recording function to create the accompanying audio. When students arrived at each station, they could both read and listen to the multi-step directions.

Transitions

Let students know when they will transition during the lesson, how long the transitions will be and where they need to go after they finish work at each station. We suggest using the following tools to aid with transitions:

> » *number signs posted at each station to help students understand the order of the station rotations*
> » *a timer, buzzer or set of chimes to indicate that it is time to move to a new station*
> » *a poster or short video illustrating what the transitions should look like (include information about the length of the transition and what students should do with any materials they are collecting or using at each individual station)*

Materials

Some teachers ask students to complete products at various stations as evidence of their participation and learning. Students might be asked to write a quick reflection, add to a collaborative list or shoot a video detailing something they learned. These products are easy to incorporate into a station teaching lesson but do not need to be used at any or all of them. Again, the activities will depend on your lesson objectives and student needs.

If you are asking students to create products during your lessons, be sure to design a way to collect them. You might, for instance, ask for electronic submissions or leave wire baskets at each station.

Differentiating Stations

There may be countless ways to personalize learning by using stations, but we suggest paying special attention to how co-teaching can help you serve and support your diverse learners. For example, you can vary the personal supports you provide at stations. Sometimes you may both want to teach mini-lessons at different stations. On another day, you may both want to facilitate the station teaching lesson so you can engage in observations of learning. On yet other days, you may vary roles so that one of you is working with individual students during the lesson and the other is primarily facilitating the entire activity.

Of course, there are many more ways you can differentiate using a stations teaching model. We offer a few ideas here:

» *Allow students to choose which stations to visit or offer choices within stations (e.g. read a passage or watch a video).*
» *Provide a range of materials at some or all stations so students have a variety of ways to learn and show what they know.*
» *Label one station as the enrichment/discovery station and let all students who finish their work visit this station or assign some students to skip certain stations and move to that station early.*
» *Ask students with exceptional skills or abilities in certain areas to design their own stations and facilitate activities at those stations.*

» Ask students for ideas on how to make the station lessons more challenging, relevant or interesting.

» Give some students opportunities to spend all of their time at one station working on a specific independent project.

» Assign one teacher the role of enrichment specialist. This person should check in with various students and provide them with discussion opportunities or more challenging content.

» Assign one teacher the role of support specialist. This person should check in with struggling students and provide them with any necessary cues, materials or strategies.

» Have some students take on leadership roles within some of the stations. These individuals can offer support to those needing it, demonstrate a skill or show off products they have created.

TO DO LIST

☐ Get on the "station wagon"! Develop a lesson plan for a station teaching model and teach the lesson.

☐ Discuss the lesson. How did it go? What would you have to tweak to use this model again?

☐ Consider the ideas offered for differentiating instruction in a station teaching model. Try one of these ideas to support students with unique learning profiles in your classroom.

TABLE 16.2
Station Teaching Examples

 ### Reading/Literacy: Kindergarten

A Kindergarten teacher and a speech pathologist regularly co-teach during language arts lessons. During a lesson on "how things grow," three stations were used. The speech pathologist read two books about gardening at station one. At station two, students independently wrote in their journals about what they learned about growing food at a trip to a farm. At station three, students engaged in a scientific exploration of seeds and recorded observations in journals.

 ### Math: Middle School

Four stations are used regularly by a middle school math team. One of the stations changes throughout the year, but the three constants are the teacher-led station where the general education teacher introduces new content to a small group of students, the tech table where students practice a recently learned concept using a game on a popular math website and the group challenge station where students work together to solve a complex problem. The special education teacher in this classroom is the station facilitator; his job is to check with students at all stations, to answer questions and to keep the rotations moving smoothly and on time. Some students rotate through all of the stations, but others visit only one or two, repeating some stations for purposes of reinforcement or enrichment.

 ### Music: Middle School

Four stations are occasionally used in a middle school music class. One is designed for listening to recordings of music (e.g., African drumming, jazz solos), one for collaboratively composing music, one for learning a new skill and one for researching artists, events and other related material on the web. Sometimes the music teacher facilitates the stations and students participate in each activity independently. Other times, however, the lessons are co-taught and the music teacher works with students on their compositions while a special educator acts as a facilitator, engages in observations or takes data on student IEP objectives.

 ### Social Studies: High School

Stations are often used by one co-taught social studies team to introduce new units. At one teacher-led station, students are required to engage in close readings of primary documents related to the new content. The other teacher leads a second station where students look at artifacts or take a virtual fieldtrip to a location related to upcoming lessons. At a third station, students typically have to engage in some type of informal research. This is usually an independent learning station, but it is sometimes led by the school's library assistant.

 ### French: High School

Five stations are used each Friday in a high school French class. The themes of the stations stay constant throughout the year. One station is a conversation station where students talk to their French teacher and a few peers in French. Another station is a kiddie lit station where students work alone or with partners to translate picture books into English. At a third station, students work on their writing with an interactive software program. At the fourth station, students practice vocabulary words using any one of three different methods. At the fifth station, students complete workbook exercises. Since there are several students on the autism spectrum in this classroom, a special educator occasionally co-teaches with the French teacher. He typically spends time supporting students as they play the vocabulary games and access the software program.

TABLE 16.3

Wise & Well-Crafted Responses to Station Teaching Objections

Objections to station teaching	Wise and well-crafted responses to station teaching objections
"We don't have enough room for two teachers to conduct stations."	Many teachers use station teaching inside the classroom but you can also engineer a station teaching model by tapping into alternative instructional spaces. Can one group go outside? To the library? To a nearby classroom? If you cannot leave the classroom, you can still engage in station teaching. Just be sure to teach guidelines about voice volume, transitions and behavior (e.g., stay with your group). Use table spaces, rugs, clusters of desks and so on to create stations. Keep in mind that not all stations need desks or even spaces. If one station requires students to snap photos of geometric shapes, these learners might be turned loose in the hallway (with one supervising teacher, of course) for that purpose.
"I don't know how to divide the content for stations."	There are many ways to divide content; teachers should feel free to use the method that best fits the material and the learning needs of students. Some teachers create stations based on the multiple intelligences (Gardner, 1983). For instance, they may have a bodily-kinesthetic station, a verbal-linguistic station and a logical-mathematical station; this method ensures that all students (or at least most) get to learn in a way that is most appealing to them. Another method of dividing content is to plan around resources and materials (e.g., teacher-led center, iPad center, microscope exploration center). Still other teachers use station teaching as a way to differentiate the difficulty of content. These educators might feature an enrichment station, a review station and a choice station in their rotations.
"Voices get too loud and the room gets too chaotic when we use stations."	Chaotic moments can occur during any sort of active learning experience, but this does not mean we need to limit these sorts of lessons. Instead, incorporate some chaos-management techniques into your station teaching model: • Play soft music and ask students to monitor their voices so that the music can be heard. • Create some silent stations (e.g., watching a video clip with headphones, annotating a document, blogging). • Use a "whisper" signal. • Physically position stations as far enough away from one another as possible. • Ask students for noise-reduction ideas.
"It is disruptive to move materials and seats. We lose valuable instructional time as students move from station to station."	This is a reasonable objection, but we feel that the benefits of station teaching outweigh this drawback. To mitigate this challenge, take concrete steps to aid transitions and maximize time-on-task: • Work with students on seamless transitions. Ask them for assistance. Shoot some video of a less-than-successful transition and have students provide feedback on how to make improvements. • Teach students how to transition. Use visuals such as number signs and arrows to indicate how and where they should move. • Present clear directions for each station so students can begin working the minute they arrive at a new work space.
"It is overwhelming to assess all of the products that students create during a station teaching lesson."	This is a common concern. Many teachers believe that every station needs to be connected to the development of a product. You can create stations that require the development of or contribution to a product, but no station needs to be tied to an assessable item. Keep in mind that a high-quality station teaching lesson does not require students to keep busy. It does, however, require that they are immersed in meaningful work and learning key concepts. For example, a station teaching lesson that requires students to watch and discuss a Kahn Academy (www.khanacademy.org) video at one station, engage in a probability dice game at another station and review a lesson on probability with a teacher at a third station is varied and engaging; gives students opportunities to address key skills; and does not necessarily result in the creation of a single product.

DAY 17

WATCH & LEARN

One of the co-teaching structures that often gets forgotten in the bustle of the busy school year is one teach/one observe. Teachers may not see the need for observation when they have so much going on in terms of planning curriculum, delivering instruction and assessing learners, but it is hard for teams to grow in skill and ability if they don't take time to look around the classroom, "kidwatch" and evaluate their practices. Therefore, we are going to use every inch of the next few pages to help you focus on the importance of this underutilized co-teaching structure.

Does My Pumpkin-Scarecrow-Candycorn Sweater Clash With My New Leopard-Print Clipboard?

In most aspects of life, we can all profit from an honest assessment every once in a while. If you have ever unknowingly dry-erased the whiteboard with your backside, you know what we mean. Whether you want help collaborating more effectively with the therapists on your team, figuring out whether or not you need more navy-blue Sharpies in your desktop collection or determining if the fluorescent lights cast you in a flattering hue, you should be able to turn to your co-teacher for support.

If you have developed a strong partnership, your co-teacher should be able to play various roles in your professional life and vice versa. Sometimes, you will need your partner to serve as a coach of sorts. Other times, you will just need a sounding board. Still other times, you will need to turn to your co-teacher to evaluate your work. Observer may be one of the most important roles you adopt, but it can also be one of the most challenging. Evaluation can feel intimidating—kind of like stepping under or behind a giant magnifying glass—but it can also be an incredibly useful way to help improve classroom practice.

Who Am I Watching & What Should I See?

Most co-teachers who utilize one teach/one observe do so routinely as a way to reach a targeted goal. Therefore, observation is not usually done for an entire day or even an entire lesson. Instead this structure will likely result in the best outcomes when used (a) on a weekly or monthly basis for short segments of time (five to fifteen minutes), and (b) to focus on particular aspects of your practice or of student behavior.

What to observe will vary from team to team as the feedback you seek will likely be connected to personal goals, student goals or district and state goals. We suggest that all teams consider using at least two kinds of observations across the school year—student observation and teacher observation.

Student Observation

At times, it will be useful for one teacher in your partnership to take a step out of the instructional role and simply observe learners in the classroom. This can help both of you attend to student behaviors that are hard to study in any meaningful way when you are in the midst of creating *Romeo and Juliet* puppet shows with twenty-six teenagers. You can either target the behaviors of all students (appropriate when a particular group of students seem to be struggling or when a group is challenging to both of you in any way) or just one or two students who may have needs and goals that require ongoing assessment. When engaged in student-focused observations, it can be helpful to give both in the partnership a chance to serve in this role for a period of time so that the dynamic between students and each individual teacher can be taken into account. For instance, if one of you seems to be more effective at supporting a student with emotional needs, you can explore why that might be happening and use that knowledge to better support not only that student, but potentially others in the classroom as well.

One teach/one observe is particularly useful when you have students with disabilities in your classroom who require regular assessment of individual social, communication, behavior or academic skills. However, we feel this practice can be helpful to every teacher, no matter the needs of his or her students, so keep in mind that there are many different behaviors that you may want to take time to observe. See Table 17.1 for student observation ideas.

TABLE 17.1
One Teach/One Observe: Student Behaviors

» communication skills (e.g., making on-target contributions to discussions)

» social skills (e.g., turn taking, using appropriate voice volume)

» academic skills (e.g., reading fluently)

» use of learning tools (e.g., completing a graphic organizer, working with manipulatives)

» use of curricular adaptations (e.g., following a visual checklist, using note-taking software)

Teacher Observation

The second application for one teach/one observe is using it to provide feedback for your partner. For instance, a team might set a goal of increasing student involvement during whole-class discussion and lecture. Co-teaching partners might then observe one another to (a) ensure that each teacher is meeting the goal, and (b) informally evaluate the impact of any teaching changes that have been made (e.g., pausing to allows students to "turn and talk"). Observation can also be used to address certain course and content goals. For example, one team we know set a goal to improve their Socratic questioning techniques. They use the following questions as guidelines in observation:

> » *Was the goal for the discussion made clear?*
> » *Did the teacher respond to most/many answers with a question?*
> » *Did the teacher question inferences, interpretations and conclusions where appropriate? (e.g., "What did you mean by that?")*
> » *Did the teacher stay focused on key ideas and concepts?*
> » *Did the teacher examine point of view?*
> » *Did the teacher call for more precision or greater detail when needed?*
> » *Were adaptations for Rachel and Harrison in place (e.g., cue cards)? Did Harrison seem to have a way to participate in the discussion? Did Rachel and Harrison participate in the discussion?*

See Table 17.2 for teacher observation ideas.

TABLE 17.2
One Teach/One Observe: Teacher Behaviors

» emphasizing/reinforcing key lesson objectives

» calling on boys & girls equally

» providing clear directions

» giving clear demonstrations

» pacing lessons appropriately

» modeling learning strategies (e.g., questioning, annotating)

» integrating assistive technology (AT) into the lesson

» using total physical response (TPR) strategies

» providing wait time before asking students to respond

» encouraging student exploration/ questioning

» creating opportunities for students with disabilities to participate in lesson/ discussion

» providing feedback

» avoiding the use of nuisance words (e.g., *like, uh, um*)

» providing direct or indirect support to certain students

» encouraging peer interaction and support

» addressing IEP objectives during lesson/ providing enrichment opportunities during lesson

» using more than one mode of output during lesson

» teaching to more than one or two of the multiple intelligences

---

Two Teach/Two Observe

Do you like the idea of observing, but hate the notion of being apart from your co-teaching partner for even one lesson? We have you covered. We feel that one teach/one observe is invaluable to the professional development of co-teachers, but we acknowledge that sometimes it may actually be most appropriate to engage in observations as you teach: together.

When we started our teaching careers, it was a challenge to video record in the classroom. You had to go to the AV department, check out a camera, learn how to use it by reading a seventy-eight-page manual, find a space to plug it in and hope the lesson was still going on by the time you were ready to press "record." Have times ever changed! Today, most of us have video cameras on our phones and carry our recording devices in our book bags, backpacks and back pockets. Now, two teach/ two observe is almost as easy as its solo counterpart. You simply set up your camera and shoot a lesson. Then, edit your video to highlight the pieces you want to target in your observation. Now you can use the footage not only to evaluate your work, but potentially to demonstrate to others (e.g., administrators, parents) the awesomeness of your co-teaching partnership.

How Can These Observations Change Your Life (Or At Least Positively Influence Your Teaching)?

Getting data about how you are doing is very much like stepping on a scale for the purpose of weight loss. The number you see in the window can be helpful, but only if you do something with the information. If the news is positive, you can take steps to continue to see positive outcomes and possibly even work toward a loftier goal. If the news is not so great, that's okay. You have taken an important step by just participating in the observation. Now you can take that data and make improvements based on what you have learned. Start by talking to your partner about your findings. Then revisit the goals of the observation. Address the specific behaviors you targeted. Finally, you can expand the discussion and touch on other related issues.

Consider the following questions to get you started:

> » *How did I do on the specific behaviors (e.g., eliciting responses, pacing the lesson) I asked you to observe?*
> » *What struck you about the behavior/performance of specific students in this lesson?*
> » *How did the students do on any specific behaviors we targeted in this observation?*
> » *What evidence of student learning did you observe?*
> » *What went well?*
> » *What did you notice?*
> » *What surprised you?*
> » *Have you noticed improvement in any skills/competencies we have targeted?*
> » *What changes do we need to make?*
> » *What questions do you have?*

Don't be shy about including playful and positive questions.

For student observations, you might ask:

» *What did he/she do that impressed you?*
» *Did the student/s observed make great progress, amazing progress or unspeakable progress since our last observation?*
» *Did anything mind-blowing occur in the observation? Did anything make you beam with pride?*
» *How lucky are these students to have us as teachers?*

For teacher observations, you might ask:

» *If today's observation was a feature film, which moment would give me the Oscar?*
» *Which students were hanging on my every word? Which students almost left the room? Did anyone actually leave the room?*
» *On a scale of 1–10, how jaw-dropping/dazzling/mind-blowing was this lesson?*
» *How can I improve my organization? The lesson introduction? My outfit?*

Hey! You may roll your eyes at these, but we have found that asking and answering the aforementioned questions can be fun and maybe even make less-positive feedback easier to hear. Further, you may end up with ideas for adding a pop of color to your mostly-neutral-toned wardrobe. So, be brave, start with the positives and proceed to share, discuss and learn.

TO DO LIST

☐ Schedule three observation sessions today—one for you, one for your co-teaching partner and one for students.

☐ Schedule your feedback sessions.

☐ Repeat until you are the best and most fiercely co-observed co-teaching classroom on the planet.

DIFFERENTIATE FOR ALL

Remember being a student back in the '60s, '70s or '80s? You don't? My goodness! Co-teachers are getting younger all the time. Well, if you don't remember the good old days, let us paint you a picture. The teacher typically stood at the front of the classroom, delivering lessons to students who were expected to receive that instruction passively. Sometimes it worked. Sometimes it did not. Material may have been learned for a short period of time but was often forgotten almost as quickly as it was taught. And differentiation? There was a bit of that. Some teachers may have used books on tape or experimented with technology (read: electric typewriters). Others may have provided a little enrichment support by allowing unfettered access to the SRA Reading Laboratory or by assigning the occasional project. In other words, differentiation as we know it today was rare.

This is not to say that those of us educated "back in the day" did not receive a high quality education. We may have learned a bit more if we had access to some of the methods and materials available today, but many of us did have a positive schooling experience because our teachers cared about us and creatively used the resources available to them. Those resources may not have been sufficient, however, for students with certain learning differences. Many struggled mightily in classrooms of yore.

Thankfully, the field of education has changed. Today, we not only have a host of technologies and materials helping us respond to differences, we also have permission to abandon the front of the classroom and allow students to be at the center of their own learning.

Today, we will explore five ways co-teaching teams can move away from traditional lesson design and differentiate by letting students take over. We love all of these ideas for the co-taught classroom, because while they are ideal ways to differentiate, they can be hard for one teacher to manage and require a lot of coaching, listening and collaboration with students. All five of these structures can be used across grade levels and will help any team personalize curriculum and instruction.

Curriculum Compacting

Curriculum compacting allows teachers to streamline what is taught to students by first assessing their prior knowledge (by administering a short quiz, for example) and then eliminating or adapting work that has already been mastered. This technique is a form of content acceleration that enables some students to skip work that is not appropriately challenging and access content that is. Students who have not yet mastered the material proceed with planned activities. Students who have mastered some of the upcoming material might move through the content more quickly and then engage in an enrichment activity. Students who have mastered all of the upcoming material may immediately work on an independent project or consult with a mentor or cross-age tutor.

The goals of compacting are to create a challenging learning environment, guarantee proficiency in basic curriculum and buy time for enrichment and acceleration (Reis & Renzulli, 1992). According to Reis and Renzulli, the following eight steps of compacting are key:

> » *Determine objectives for the unit of study.*
> » *Find or create a way to assess competencies and knowledge related to these objectives.*
> » *Identify students who may have mastered the objectives or have the potential to master them at a faster than typical pace.*
> » *Pretest students on one or more of the objectives.*
> » *Streamline practice, drill or instructional time for students who have learned the objectives.*
> » *Provide instructional options for students who have not yet attained all the pre-tested objectives but generally learn faster than their classmates.*
> » *Organize and recommend enrichment or acceleration options for eligible students.*

» *Keep records of the process and instructional options available to students whose curriculum has been compacted for reporting to parents, and forward these records to next year's teachers.*

Keep in mind that this technique can also be adapted for students needing more support in a given unit of study. If teachers determine that pieces of upcoming lessons are not appropriate for the targeted learner, educators can follow the same steps outlined above but provide curricular options that are less challenging instead of more challenging.

An example of compacting was observed in one high school English classroom where a teaching team routinely used it to study novels. If learners had read the book, could clearly communicate their understanding of targeted concepts and could test out of the material, they were allowed to select from a menu of options related to the content (see Table 18.1).

TABLE 18.1

Compacting Options for Students Needing Enrichment:
To Kill a Mockingbird [TKAM]

» Write a modern day screenplay based on the events in the novel.

» Engage in an independent study of the Scottsboro cases (Lee's inspiration for the trial in *TKAM*). Include an exploration of the related Supreme Court cases in your investigation.

» Choose a nonfiction book to read to expand your knowledge of race and the law in this country (e.g., *The Children*). Be prepared to share your learning with the class in some way.

» Design a children's book based on a theme from the novel.

» Do an author study on Harper Lee. Read literary criticism of *TKAM*.

» Collect an oral history from someone who lived through the Jim Crow era. Work with your teachers to decide on a participant and on your methodology. Choose at least one way to share your interview (e.g., write a report for the local newspaper, share a video clip on the classroom blog).

Using a similar process, students with identified disabilities were allowed to "compact" out of parts of the unit when teacher-created assessments suggested that the material might either be too complex or too abstract for them. These learners were also allowed to choose from a list of options similar to those offered to students needing more challenge (see Table 18.2).

TABLE 18.2

Compacting Options for Students Needing Support:
To Kill a Mockingbird [TKAM]

» Engage in an independent study of any one of these topics:

- lawyers/trials
- civil rights
- African-American history

» Interview a lawyer; ask him or her to explain human and civil rights.

» Choose a book on race relations in the United States (e.g., *We've Got a Job: The 1963 Birmingham Children's March*). Read or listen to the book and choose a way to report on your learning.

» Make a short movie or write/illustrate a short book on doing what is right.

WHY WE LOVE IT IN A CO-TAUGHT CLASSROOM

When two teachers are available to teach and manage lessons, keeping track of learners who are compacting becomes much easier. We recommend designating one person in your partnership to keep records of students who are working on alternative goals and facilitate those experiences. The other should be responsible for leading lessons for the rest of the class.

Tic-Tac-Toe

Tic-tac-toe is ideal for the differentiated classroom as it gives all students the opportunity to study the same material as their classmates without having to follow a prescribed set of activities or learning experiences. In other words, these game boards allow every learner in the classroom to study the material in a completely unique way.

Different teachers may have different rules for using tic-tac-toe boards, but most ask students to complete three tasks diagonally, down a column or across a row. Some teachers require all students to use the middle square so that there will be one common assignment in the unit. This rule does not apply to the tic-tac-toe game students typically play, so you will want to be sure to explain expectations clearly the first time you use this activity in the classroom.

To create your tic-tac-toe board, identify the outcomes and instructional focus of a unit of study. Then, use data, observations, conversations with learners and student profiles to determine the needs, learning styles and interests in your classroom. After you have this information, design nine different tasks that will both address lesson goals and honor student preferences. While you arrange the tasks on the board, keep in mind that if you do require every student to use the center square, this task should be the most critical for all to experience.

Want to adapt this structure for your diverse learners? There are many ways to make tic-tac-toe more or less complex. For instance, you might let students work in teams, challenge some learners to complete certain tasks instead of others or keep one square open for anyone wanting to design their own learning experience.

See Figure 18.1 for an example of a tic-tac-toe board used in a biology class.

FIGURE 18.1:
Tic-Tac-Toe Board: Cell Unit

Create a card game about cells based on a popular game others know (Uno, Old Maid, Go Fish); play 3 games with at least 2 classmates.	Create a 3-D model of a cell using any materials you choose.	Complete a special project designed by you & approved by Ms. Grant or Ms. Yoshina: _____ _____ _____
Create a detailed graphic organizer comparing and contrasting a plant cell and an animal cell.	Read pp. 68-78 in the textbook and create a written summary of key points or use www.smore.com to make a flyer about the content.	Make a crossword puzzle using these words: *cell wall, nucleus, organelle, cell membrane, chloroplast* and 8 other terms from the unit that you choose. The clues should not be lifted straight from the definitions in the textbook. Instead, try to stump the solver and show off your understanding of the terms.
Read *The Immortal Life of Henrietta Lacks* by Rebecca Skloot & write a review of it on Goodreads (www.goodreads.com).	Create a fictional Facebook account for your favorite cell. Include at least 7 posts and 3 photos.	Design and perform an experiment about cells with your lab partner. Be sure to write a complete lab report.

WHY WE LOVE IT IN A CO-TAUGHT CLASSROOM

Teachers often resist using activities like tic-tac-toe because they require a lot of supervision, coaching and conversation with students. The constant flurry of activity can be overwhelming for one teacher. Two teachers, however, can split the class in half and each can take responsibility for managing the activities of a smaller group of learners. We recommend this discrete split because teachers can immerse themselves in the work of their designated students without worrying that their co-teaching partner has already asked the same questions, taken the same data or given the same cues or reminders.

Learning Plans

Learning plans are teacher-created lists of projects or activities that must be completed during a specific period of time, usually during a unit of study. Typically, students work independently on their plans, asking for support when needed and collaborating with other learners when necessary (Schwarz & Kluth, 2007).

Learning plans help students visually track the work that needs completing and the activities they have already finished. Students using plans, therefore, can develop management and organizational skills as they are learning the targeted content.

The tasks on learning plans should vary according to student needs. In one classroom, for instance, all students had the same agenda for a unit on anatomy (e.g., make diagrams of each system, read chapter 7) but some learners had extra items for enrichment (e.g., interview the school nurse or a physician you know about health occupations) and one student had an item related to her IEP goal of using the telephone (e.g., call your doctor and ask for information on preventative health).

See Figure 18.2 for examples of learning plans for a fractions unit.

FIGURE 18.2
Learning Plans: Fractions Unit

Kasi

» Complete the first 2 pages in our workbook.

» Complete a lesson with Ms. Sanchez.

» Watch the "Fraction Shuffle" rap video again.

» Play the Fraction Flags game 3x for 10-15 minutes each: www.maths-games.org/fraction-games.html.

Madeline

» Complete all 3 pages in our workbook.

» Complete a lesson with Ms. Merris.

» Grab a recipe from our box. Write a new version where you triple the recipe.

» Play the Fraction Flags game if you have time: www.maths-games.org/fraction-games.html.

Abe

» Complete all 3 pages in our workbook.

» Complete a lesson with Ms. Merris.

» Create a 5-10 minute video tutorial (à la www.learnzillion.com) teaching your classmates how to reduce fractions to their simplest form.

WHY WE LOVE IT IN A CO-TAUGHT CLASSROOM

Learning agendas allow teachers to address so many different goals in the same unit. In a co-teaching model, we like to use one teacher as the ringleader during this work and the other as the director of a key activity. The ringleader typically serves in many roles (e.g., keeping students on task, answering questions), while the other teacher usually provides instruction and guidance to individual students or small groups (e.g., reteaching material).

Anchor Activities

Anchor activities are tasks that students can work on independently or at least without teacher support. These activities may be assigned when students walk into the classroom or they can simply be implemented for some period during a class to give teachers time to observe students, engage in individual assessments or meet with small groups. In essence, anchor activities free teachers from their work as classroom "directors" or facilitators and allow them to designate valuable class time for more personalized interactions with learners.

True anchor activities should always be meaningful and allow students to deepen their understanding of learning standards and lesson objectives. They should also allow each student to work at a different pace and on different content (if necessary or desired), which is why they are ideal to use in a differentiated classroom. The only requirements of anchor activities are that they must be (a) worthy of a student's time, (b) appropriate to his or her abilities and (c) easy to "enter" and "exit" so that transitions are short.

Some teachers are reluctant to have students work on desktop tasks or independent activities because they view time that isn't teacher-directed as wasted. When anchor activities are carefully planned, however, nothing could be further from the truth. This independent work can give students opportunities to be self-directed, to demonstrate initiative and to give and get support from peers.

An example of how anchors can buy co-teachers quality time with students comes from the tenth-grade social studies class of Ms. Watts and Mr. Philbin. In this classroom, anchor activities are used for the first twenty minutes of each Friday class. The anchor changes weekly and the directions are posted so that students can begin work immediately upon entering the classroom. The anchor may be silent or partner reading, work on an ongoing project or exploration of resources on a teacher-selected website. The only rule is that the learners must rely on one another for support.

One thing that doesn't change is what the teachers are doing. Ms. Watts and Mr. Philbin always use this time to meet with individual students in the class. Ms. Watts, the general education teacher, conducts short conferences with small groups, giving them direction on how to enhance their ongoing projects. Students work on the projects for over three months. The experience culminates with the groups creating resources (e.g., websites, interactive bulletin boards, short subject videos) to teach others about a topic related to human rights (e.g., hunger in America, inclusive education, racism). Mr. Philbin sits in on some of the conferences to learn more about the content but also to teach or assess IEP-related skills (e.g., topic maintenance). Occasionally, the teachers both pull groups of students to coach and support. If necessary, Mr. Philbin may take a break from the conferences to keep the students "anchored" on the assigned activities.

 WHY WE LOVE IT IN A CO-TAUGHT CLASSROOM

Typically (in a classroom that is not co-taught), anchor activities require students to work independently. This is a challenge for some groups of students and for very young students, so when a teacher is available to supervise the "anchoring" activity, students can still work on their own, but support is available if needed. If your students don't need supervision, that's even better. Now you have two teachers pulling individuals and small groups. Use this time not only to provide instruction, but also to listen to your learners. They will undoubtedly have a lot to say once they have your undivided attention.

Personalized Learning Agendas

Educators have been focused on differentiating instruction for years, but methods that give students true autonomy are rare. For this reason, we recommend that teachers in diverse classrooms embrace the personal learning agenda (Kluth & Danaher, 2013) as a tool for teaching to differences.

Personalized learning agendas look a lot like pages out of a daily planner or calendar (see Figure 18.3). Broken into small chunks of time (e.g., ten- or fifteen-minute blocks), they allow students to choose activities they will engage in to meet the goals of a unit or to study a targeted subject. Using this tool, students can, in essence, write their own lesson plans for a period of time.

FIGURE 18.3
Learning Agenda: Example

LEARNING AGENDA

Name:_____

Keep in mind:

» You should schedule in ¼ hour blocks. With approval, you may extend segments.
» Your agenda must be approved by a teacher.
» One segment must be dedicated to writing or editing.

	activity	proposed outcome	teacher notes
8:00 - 8:15			
8:15 - 8:30			
8:30 - 8:45			
8:45 - 9:00			
9:00 - 9:15			

To begin, decide when you will use your agendas. Some teachers start by using them for an hour or so each week and then expand to longer periods of time.

At first, let students plan just one or two activities. Many learners will have endless ideas for using their agendas, but some will struggle mightily with this open-ended task. To set all students up for success, be sure to provide clear lists of activities to choose from, as well as guidance on how to best manage the time they are given.

Then, develop a procedure for evaluating agendas. Will you have them submit their forms for approval? Will you glance at their choices as you circulate during independent work time? How will you assess their progress and productivity? These questions might be answered in one way when you introduce agendas and then revised and updated after you have seen the agendas in action.

In one eighth-grade language arts class, students worked off of learning agendas every Friday. Agendas had to be approved by a teacher each week, and progress and completed work had to be documented. The classroom was co-taught both days so teachers could spend time reviewing proposed activities, supporting individuals and small groups and providing feedback on ongoing work. During this time, students might be reading independently, conferencing with peers or teachers, completing unfinished assignments or learning a new skill (e.g., writing an epic poem, using the Kurzweil Reader, creating an infographic).

 WHY WE LOVE IT IN A CO-TAUGHT CLASSROOM

As you add more personal support into the classroom, the possibilities for agendas really soar. With one adult, the teacher may have to occasionally turn down student requests (e.g., Can I spend some time outside doing observations for my insect project?; Can someone teach me how to use the darkroom?; Can we do a survey with the parents in the family center?) because of a lack of resources, expertise or supervision. When you have more than one teacher available, however, a wider range of student ideas become possible. To really create rich and memorable agenda lessons, don't limit your collaboration to the co-teaching partnership. This is a great time to bring in mentors, volunteers, community experts, therapists and administrators to teach, provide support and inspire creativity.

TO DO LIST

- [ ] Start small. Determine a subject or time of day where the academic spread is wide. Select one of the five ideas in this section and make a plan to differentiate for all.

- [ ] Don't stop there. Keep going. Choose another.

- [ ] Try one more. You're on a roll, y'all!

DAY 19

TRY 10 FOR 2

By now you must be thinking, "Okay, okay...I'm sold on all of that stuff about co-teaching rationale, roles, meeting information, differentiating instruction and the like...but when do I get to learn more about hunting for cylinders, felling the Berlin Wall and honoring Oprah? You are in luck. On Day 19, we feel you are ready to think about some of the exciting lesson format possibilities in the co-taught classroom. Yesterday, you explored differentiation strategies for turning the learning over to students. Today, you will expand on that knowledge base and add ten new ideas to your bag of teaching tricks. These ideas are not quite as open-ended and student-driven as those we featured in Day 18, but they will nevertheless help you punch up a traditional lesson and give it a bit of energy, spirit and razzle-dazzle.

If you are co-teaching, it is the best possible time to take risks with your instruction and bring some innovation into your lesson plans and your classroom. In fact, we often say that if you are not teaching differently and using a wider range of approaches than you did before your partner arrived, you are not really co-teaching.

Why Use A Range Of Formats?

According to Holt (1967), learning is enhanced when students can state information in their own words, make use of it in a myriad of ways and recognize it in various forms and circumstances. Using different types of lesson formats is one strategy that creates opportunities for students to learn in these diverse ways.

Udvari-Solner (1996) defined lesson format as the "infrastructure of architecture upon which the learning experience is built." She explains that, "the organizational framework, methods to impart information to the students, and ways in which students interact with that information are all elements of lesson format" (p. 248). When teachers use a wide variety of formats and decrease their reliance on lecture, whole-class discussion and "raise and respond" structures, many students feel more comfortable sharing and participating. Further, when those formats allow students to be more active and engaged, performance is enhanced. In a study on alternatives to the lecture, researchers found that students in active learning classrooms failed less often and got higher test scores than those in traditional classrooms (Freeman, Eddy, McDonough, Smith, Okoroafor, Jordt & Wenderoth, 2014).

This need for responsive lesson formats may be even more significant for those with unique learning profiles. Temple Grandin (1995), a woman on the autism spectrum with a doctorate in animal science, recalls that she learned the most when teachers allowed her to actively participate in lessons:

> I vividly remember learning about the solar system by drawing it on the bulletin board and taking field trips to the science museum. Going to the science museum and doing experiments in my third- and fourth-grade classrooms made science real to me. The concept of barometric pressure was easy to understand after we made barometers out of milk bottles, rubber sheeting, and drinking straws. (p. 97)

Expanding Your Formats

In our experience, many teachers are interested in implementing complex and innovative lessons but don't always have the time and the resources to pull them off easily or effectively. In classrooms with two teachers, however, plans that seem impossible or implausible suddenly can seem not only doable but appealing.

This is not to say, of course, that these lesson ideas cannot be implemented by a single teacher. In fact, most teachers using these options today are likely doing so without a partner. What we are suggesting is that these particular formats work very well with two educators; the opportunity to collaborate during a simulation, scavenger hunt or tableau lesson makes those activities much more manageable and all the more fun.

Tableau

Imagine walking into your classroom and seeing some of your students pretending to chisel away at your classroom door, others positioned atop chairs with arms raised in the air and still others standing still as soldiers. This probably isn't a rebellion staged to communicate distaste about your last unit test. We are guessing that if you have introduced tableau into your classroom, it is probably just a reenactment of the collapse of the Berlin Wall.

In tableau, participants use their bodies to make still images. These images represent a scene, word, concept, idea or theme. Because students are "frozen" during a tableau, it is easier to manage than skits or whole-group improvisation, yet it can easily lead into extended drama activities. It can be used to explore a particular moment in a story or novel (especially useful when many characters are involved), to replicate a painting or photograph, to replay a historical moment or to visually define a word or concept. For instance, students might illustrate different ways to think about negative numbers, vocabulary words like *freedom* or *hypothesis*, various scenes from *The Book Thief*, moments from the Selma to Montgomery marches or interpretations of Seurat's *A Sunday Afternoon on the Island of La Grande Jatte*.

Tableau can be easily integrated into a range of lessons. If your students have not had much exposure to drama, it is the perfect introduction to the performing arts as it requires no speaking or movement (in fact, both are forbidden) and inspires students to collaborate.

 WHY WE LOVE IT IN A CO-TAUGHT CLASSROOM

Two teachers simply add to the drama and splendor of tableau. One teacher can facilitate groups as they perform and analyze other groups, while the other teacher captures the event on video, uses the camera to interview students about the process and the content or snaps photos of each scene. The footage captured can serve as an informal assessment tool.

WebQuests

A WebQuest (Dodge, 1995) is a collaborative, inquiry-oriented lesson format in which most or all of the information that students access comes from the Internet. This structure is designed to make web learning efficient. A typical web search involves as many misses as hits. That is, some sites that students find may be reputable and have relevant information and others may not. In a WebQuest, however, "surfing" is not necessary; students can skip the browsing process and spend their time on the web reading, learning and creating.

WebQuests are fairly easy to set up. Teachers pose problems for teams of students to solve and then direct them to research solutions online. The process is intended to encourage students to explore a wide range of perspectives, materials and resources, and inspire them to think differently, learn more authentically and potentially even create products that spark new questions. For example, Cynthia Matzat's Radio Days (www.thematzats.com/radio) takes students back in time to the 1930s and 1940s by having them create a radio play. By connecting learners directly to sound clips, broadcasts and radio scripts, students have enough structure to be successful in the task, but plenty of freedom to create something unique. This project is not just a "gather the facts" experience; it is clearly designed to encourage innovation and to allow students to teach and learn from each other.

A WebQuest commonly consists of the following elements:

1. *THE INTRODUCTION. This usually frames the problem, challenge or task for the learner. Sometimes the task is set up as a fictional quest of sorts. For instance, "You are an artist creating a sculpture for a new monument in Washington, DC" or "You are an assistant to Thomas Edison and you need to promote his new invention."*

2. *THE TASK. The task should be open-ended. You want students to explore, to be inventive and to move beyond seeking one correct answer. A sample task for fourth graders studying the history, economy and landmarks of their state might be: "You work for the Chamber of Commerce for the state of Wisconsin. Tourism is down. Your task is to learn what makes our state unique and design a brochure to tempt potential travelers to visit."*

3. *THE PROCESS. Learners need to know how to accomplish the task. Outline each step to be followed, share ideas for organizing information and, potentially, provide suggestions on the "how" of collaborative work. The resources should also be part of the process. Many (though not necessarily all) of the resources should be available at the click of the mouse,*

but it is fine to offer off-line resources as well. WebQuests can prompt students to examine print resources (e.g., "read page 44 of your textbook"), explore maps and other artifacts and contact experts or others who may be able to offer helpful information (e.g., "interview someone who watched the moon landing on television").

4. **THE EVALUATION.** *This part of the WebQuest outlines how the experience will be assessed. Evaluation is often in the form of a rubric, but any number of tools can be used for this purpose.*

5. **THE CONCLUSION.** *The final step of the process involves reflection and summarization. At this point it is helpful to talk to students about both the content of the lesson and the WebQuest itself. Questions might focus on what they learned, how they learned and suggestions they have for improving the process or for extending their learning.*

WHY WE LOVE IT IN A CO-TAUGHT CLASSROOM

WebQuests work well in a co-taught classroom because they allow both educators to teach, assess and work with a variety of students. Too often, one teacher functions as the "lead" while the other takes up the assistant role. In a WebQuest lesson, however, there is no need for a lead teacher so both educators are free to coach, support and provide instruction. We suggest that both teachers work with teams during WebQuests, but that each educator adopt a specific focus. For instance, one of you could focus on providing support for teams or students needing more resources or additional cues and the other could provide enrichment opportunities for those needing extra challenge.

Simulations

Teaching how a bill becomes a law? Try a simulation. Let students take on roles representing the three branches of government. Have them write bills, introduce the bills to their classmates, vote on bills proposed by others and wait to see which ones pass.

This type of simulation has many benefits in a diverse and differentiated classroom. It helps educators dive deeper into the content, provides students with opportunities to practice communication and social skills and often inspires them to extend learning beyond the classroom and the textbook.

Interested in trying a simulation in your classroom? Start by researching options online or creating your own with your partner. Be sure to plan carefully; complex simulations may take longer than one class period and often have multiple steps to plan and implement. In addition to facilitating the lesson, you and your partner will need to adapt the experience to fit student needs, teach the skills necessary for the game, assess learning and evaluate the experience, in general.

WHY WE LOVE IT IN A CO-TAUGHT CLASSROOM

Simulations are a lot of work but are so much fun for both teachers and students. Co-taught classrooms are the perfect place for simulations as you can plan for one teacher to be involved in the simulation while the other serves as a facilitator of the day's events. Or each teacher can lead a different and possibly "competing" simulation (e.g., plant owners meeting and assembly line workers meeting).

Jigsaw

In Jigsaw (Aronson & Patnoe, 1997; Kagan, 1989) students in small base groups are assigned a multifaceted problem. Each member of the group selects some piece of the material or aspect of the problem on which to focus. So, in a classroom in which students are studying the twentieth century in the United States, one base group of five students might split responsibilities this way: Tom is responsible for learning about transportation advances; Mike wants to learn about wars and conflict; Evie opts to study civil rights issues; Scott chooses politics and leaders; and Lisa examines entertainment and leisure.

In all of the other base groups in the classroom, students will split responsibilities in the same way. That is, every group of five would have one student responsible for transportation, one responsible for wars and conflict, one responsible for civil rights, one responsible for politics and leaders and one responsible for entertainment and leisure.

At this point, every student needs to learn enough about his or her topic to be able to teach that content to the rest of the base group. Students do not need to do this work alone, however. They can engage in research with a new "expert" group. The expert group consists of students who are all assigned the same topic. For example, all students assigned to transportation advances meet, engage in research, gather information, become experts on the topic and rehearse their presentations together. The expert group experience is particularly useful for students who have problems gathering or organizing information on their own.

After students in the expert groups have learned the assigned content, they plan a few strategies and perhaps even create materials for teaching it to their original base group. At a given time, students rejoin their original base groups and each student teaches his or her content to the others. In this way, all students in the classroom learn all of the material.

WHY WE LOVE IT IN A CO-TAUGHT CLASSROOM

Jigsaw involves a lot of movement and several activities. In other words, there are many "moving parts." Two teachers make it manageable. Further, having an "extra" teacher in the classroom makes it possible to add on-the-spot adaptations for those who may need them. For instance, if a student with cerebral palsy requires extra support for reporting back to his or her group (e.g., visuals, programming of a device), one of his teachers can provide it.

Scavenger Hunts

Many camp counselors, scout leaders and church group organizers have used scavenger hunts to break the ice at a meeting or social gathering. It is a game that is also used in many classrooms to help teachers build a sense of community and involve all students in teaching and learning.

Scavenger hunts require small groups of students to gather objects during a set period of time. Each group receives a worksheet with a list of prompts (e.g., "Find a cylinder"; "Find something that is six feet long"; "Find something that is at least one cubic foot in size"). Students have to collaborate and think out-of-the-box for this activity, so it is usually appreciated by novelty seekers and social butterflies alike.

To make this activity a bit richer and more interesting, you can also have students hunt for people who have information, so you might add, "Find someone who can explain how to calculate area." This person has to explain the idea, show their work on the "hunt form" and sign off as an expert.

WHY WE LOVE IT IN A CO-TAUGHT CLASSROOM

Most teachers create one scavenger hunt and use this for every group in the classroom. In a co-taught classroom, however, you can create a differentiated lesson by using more than one scavenger hunt. Consider creating several different forms based on the needs, interests and areas of expertise of your students. Then "divide and conquer" to keep track of the many tasks, the potential hunting environments and—most importantly—the "hunters."

Service Learning

Service learning is valuable because it allows students to participate in projects with tangible outcomes, make real decisions, speak and be heard, make a difference in the lives of others and achieve recognition for their accomplishments (Gent, 2009). This lesson format blends meaningful and thoughtfully planned service or volunteer work with critical reflection and opportunities to meet educational goals. Having students pick up trash around the school is not service learning, it is a nice deed. However, if students study environmental problems and pollution, examine the problem locally by talking to people in the neighborhood about beautification, collect data on where trash is accumulating, draft plans to keep the school and surrounding area litter-free, clean up the school and surrounding area and then reflect on the process and discuss how grassroots work can affect a community—that would be service learning.

Yoder, Retish and Wade (1996) found that students with disabilities who participated in service learning acquire increased self-knowledge and improved communication, problem solving and social skills. Because students with learning needs, linguistically diverse backgrounds and at-risk labels often receive services within schools and communities, they are very often enthusiastic about having opportunities to provide support to others (Morris, 1992).

See Table 19.1 for a list of service learning ideas.

TABLE 19.1
Service Learning Ideas

» Create a website to educate the public about an important topic (e.g., texting while driving).

» Set up an informational display at a local library.

» Start a beautification project (e.g., plant state wildflowers).

» Adopt a billboard; create a public service announcement to post on the board.

» Research your community and target an area in need of clean-up/repair.

» Design a campaign to promote tolerance, inclusion and understanding of differences.

» Set up a web page for a non-profit agency; work with them to understand their mission, needs and constituency.

» Make a film to illuminate an injustice.

» Write and produce a play that teaches a safety lesson to other teens or children.

» Create a model or art installation to inspire or educate.

» Launch an educational program (e.g., book recycling, peer tutoring) at your school or in your community; develop a plan for both creating and sustaining the program.

» Design an orientation program for your classroom, grade or school; create materials and activities to help new students thrive.

» Create an ongoing partnership with a local senior citizen organization to help members with technology projects (e.g., setting up e-mail, uploading photos).

WHY WE LOVE IT IN A CO-TAUGHT CLASSROOM

Combining service and learning is powerful, but it can be unwieldy to conduct some projects as a group of twenty or thirty. Splitting the class into smaller sections makes these lessons more manageable; two teachers might work on two different sites or projects at the same time, or one teacher might take students into the community in small groups while the other teacher teaches a related lesson in the classroom.

Project-Based Instruction

When you ask adults to recall the most memorable learning experiences from their K–12 school days, so many of them talk about projects. Who doesn't have a memory of creating something, of hauling materials from home to school and back and of engaging in "real work" like research, design and investigation? Ahh…we can still smell the rubber cement glue drying on our diorama of a proposed major league ballpark in Appleton, WI. But we (and by "we" we mean Paula) digress.

Teachers working in diverse classrooms often turn to project-based instruction in order to provide interesting and appropriate learning experiences for all and to make sure that students have opportunities to address individual objectives in the context of daily instruction. During project-based lessons, students without identified needs can work on organizing time and materials, writing for new audiences or polishing interviewing skills. Students with disabilities can work on those same competencies and address IEP goals at the same time. Some may be able to work on new mobility skills. Others may find opportunities to practice social competencies (e.g., asking for help, giving clear directions).

To manage projects, set clear timelines and teach students how to chart their own progress and produce a final product or products. Steer your "project managers" away from copy work and passive learning and point them toward those activities that will inspire higher-order thinking and meaningful engagement. For instance, instead of asking them to submit a paper, have them design a model or produce a mural.

See Table 19.2 for a list of project-based instruction ideas.

TABLE 19.2

Project-Based Instruction Ideas

» Create a game to learn (and to help others learn) standards-based content (e.g., Race Through the Rock Cycle).

» Design and paint a mural in the school, district or community.

» Collect community stories of significant events (e.g., recollections of Chicago during the 1968 riots; memories of the eruption of Mount St. Helens).

» Create an animated short to teach, encourage or inspire other students.

» Create and publish a weekly or monthly podcast.

» Start a You Tube channel to draw attention to an important topic.

» Conduct a study.

» Start a small nonprofit or business.

» Propose an idea to the city council or school board (e.g., start an intramural sports program).

» Invent a toy.

» Design an app to solve a problem.

» Propose an outdoor classroom, a better playground or an ideal study area.

» Design an experiment.

» Research a local historical figure.

» Create a mini-museum.

 WHY WE LOVE IT IN A CO-TAUGHT CLASSROOM

So many projects, so little time to question students, provide feedback and assess learning? Not so in the co-taught classroom. When teachers collaborate during project-based lessons, it becomes easier to meet a wider range of goals and focus on a greater variety of skills. We recommend that you split roles for the best possible outcomes. For instance, one of you might focus on the projects as they relate to standards while the other is literally the "project manager" (of a group of project managers) and keeps track of student materials, timelines and related assessments.

Desktop Teaching

Who doesn't want to be the teacher? Teaching is cool. You get the big desk. You get to talk without ever getting in trouble for it. You get discounts at Barnes & Noble. This aura of goodness and flair can be passed on to students if only for a few days when you use desktop teaching in the classroom. Desktop teaching is a lesson format designed to give students the opportunity to act as both teachers and learners (Draper, 1997; Parker, 1990). This structure involves giving students individual topics and having them prepare portable presentations based on those topics.

Students teach one another in a fair-like atmosphere; half of the students in the classroom have materials set up for desktop teaching, while the remaining students move from desk to desk and from "teacher" to "teacher," participating in the lessons. The students who are teaching can rotate with the students who are learning so they have the opportunity to participate in all of the lessons prepared by their peers or you can have all of the "teachers" in one half of the class conduct their lessons at the same time. In this version, students split up to listen to desktop lessons. "Teachers" present to just one or two learners and--after a handful of minutes--students rotate to another peer's desk to hear a new presentation. This continues until all students have seen several lessons. Groups then switch roles (teachers become learners and vice versa).

Students can include visual aids, artifacts, short activities and examples in their lessons. They should be encouraged to use everything they know about best practices in teaching and learning as they present. For instance, a student in one classroom taught her classmates about the coordinate grid and graphing lines using an "under the sea" theme. She made a large blue coordinate grid to represent the sea. She then had students plot points to represent the fish and lines to represent the seaweed. Another student in the same group taught how to graph inequalities and intervals using string and M&Ms (Draper, 1997).

WHY WE LOVE IT IN A CO-TAUGHT CLASSROOM

It is a challenge to help students engineer their lessons while teaching them new presentation skills. In a co-taught classroom, however, adults can split roles and help students in two different ways. One educator can serve as the teaching coach; his or her job is to approach individual students and help them polish their presentations. The other can work with students on subject matter. During the mini-lessons, one teacher can support the teachers and the other can help the learners by encouraging them to ask questions and take notes.

Book Clubs

There are so many reasons to use book clubs in your co-taught classroom. First of all, they get students reading more widely. Learners may get exposed to authors and genres they would not choose on their own. Secondly, book clubs give students help as they learn about events, people and phenomena through different voices and perspectives. Reading about severe weather in a textbook is just not the same as reading a first-person account from a survivor of Hurricane Katrina. Finally, you should use book clubs because Oprah wants you to do so. You know she does...and you know you should listen to Oprah.

Also known as literature circles or student-led reading discussions, book clubs have the potential to create a positive and collaborative climate in classrooms and provide a low-risk learning environment for learners who might otherwise be marginalized (Kluth & Chandler-Olcott, 2007). Although there are some variations in how these groups are organized, we like the following list of characteristics from O'Donnell-Allen (2006):

- » *They are made up of small groups of readers.*
- » *They meet on a regular basis.*
- » *They engage in systematic discussion.*
- » *They discuss books (and other texts) of the members' choice.*
- » *They use a variety of open-ended response methods (e.g., journal entries, graphic organizers) to prompt extended discussion.*
- » *Their membership varies according to the desired configuration.* (pp. 1–6)

Book clubs can be used across grade levels and they can be implemented in a variety of content areas, although they are most closely associated with English language arts classrooms. We especially love using them in inclusive classrooms because there are so many ways to differentiate instruction for those with unique learning profiles. For instance, students can choose the book they want to read, they can be assigned a range of different roles to suit their needs or abilities (e.g., word wizard, story mapper) and they can use supports such as e-readers, highlighters and sticky notes to access the material more successfully.

To use book clubs:

» *Select a range of grade level appropriate titles that would appeal to different readers and interests. After talking to students about the titles, ask each of them to indicate which ones they would be interested in reading. After all learners have provided feedback, form the clubs based on the needs of each reader, student preferences and possible group dynamics.*

» *Decide on how often your clubs will meet. Then, in the initial meeting with each book club, ask students to set a reading schedule. If the clubs will meet three times, they will chunk the reading assignments down into that many parts.*

» *Determine how students will share their learning. You might have them keep journals, share reflections or even video record some of their discussions.*

» *Finally, troubleshoot any problems. Consider how to manage absent students, those who struggle to participate, et cetera.*

 WHY WE LOVE IT IN A CO-TAUGHT CLASSROOM

Book club is a structure that can create a sense of togetherness. This is important in all classrooms, but in a co-taught classroom, where you are likely to have not only a larger group of learners, but a diverse group of them, it is absolutely critical. Use book club to build connections in the classroom and beyond. While a key aspect of most book clubs is that they are led by students, teachers and significant adults such as parents, community members and other school staff can participate in the discussions, both to model their own literate thinking and to help keep the group on track. Both you and your co-teaching partner should join book clubs when possible. Rotate into different groups every time students meet so that both of you work with each group at least once. If some groups need more support, take turns joining those students.

Community Research Teams

Did you ever wish you could just get away? Use community research in your lesson plans and your wish will be granted. So, maybe this format won't help you "get away from it all," but it is sure to inspire you to move at least a block or two away from your school!

Community research is another way to teach to the many differences in your classroom (Kluth, 2000). Instead of using the school library as the primary base of information, this type of lesson format lets learners go "straight to the source" and pursue their questions through interviews, observations and collections of community artifacts.

Group research offers something for everyone in that students have choices in which topics they want to pursue and which group roles they want to adopt. This structure also enhances student collaboration and learning. Sharan and Sharan (1992) found that group research and investigation promotes cooperation and mutual assistance among students with diverse learning profiles. They also found that students engaged in group research demonstrated higher levels of academic achievement than did their peers who learned in a more traditional whole-class method.

Because library research requires fairly sophisticated reading and writing skills, some students, including those with disabilities, may struggle to engage in the required tasks. Therefore, many students stand to learn very little, if anything, from this type of data collection alone. Investigative research in the community, however, allows students to take in information visually, kinesthetically and otherwise experientially. Using the entire community as a resource base gives students with unique learning needs opportunities to pursue topics and explore environments in which they are most interested. In fact, the research experiences can be as diverse as the students themselves.

This type of research is ideal for groups of students with a variety of abilities and interests; every student can easily find his or her niche. One research project alone may involve a wide range of skills and competencies, including generating provocative questions; designing plans; securing information about important community environments and activities; making contacts (e.g., calling potential research sites) and learning to use new technology such as apps and software (e.g., video editing tools).

Interacting in the community can also provide opportunities for IEP skill development. Although interacting with peers is a useful way to practice communication and social skills, having a chance to interview a local politician or college sports star can provide special motivation to learn new greetings or try a new joke.

 WHY WE LOVE IT IN A CO-TAUGHT CLASSROOM

There is so much involved in supporting a busy group of researchers! In a co-taught classroom, adults can split roles and assess learners from more than one angle. We recommend that you target just a handful of skills that can be specifically observed and assessed (e.g., notetaking, determining credible websites/sources) and have one educator focus on how those skills will be addressed and taught. Be sure that this educator also collects data on any IEP goals that can be integrated into the research projects. The other educator can serve as the research coach and can work with individuals and small groups to manage and complete the projects themselves.

TO DO LIST

- ☐ Identify an upcoming unit where students need to learn about different topics on the same theme. Then, make a plan to use jigsaw or desktop teaching for one or more lessons in that unit.

- ☐ Identify an upcoming unit that could benefit from a bit of drama. Then, make a plan to use tableau or a simulation for one or more lessons in that unit.

- ☐ Identify an upcoming unit that lends itself to authentic problem solving and exploration. Then, make a plan to use project-based learning or service learning for one or more lessons in that unit.

- ☐ Identify an upcoming unit that centers on seeing/finding/developing artifacts related to the content. Then, make a plan to use a scavenger hunt for one or more lessons in that unit.

- ☐ Identify an upcoming unit where students could explore a topic beyond school walls. Then, make a plan to use community-based instruction for one or more lessons in that unit.

- ☐ Identify an upcoming unit where students could profit from exploring and comparing a variety of viewpoints, artifacts and/or resources. Then, make a plan to use book clubs or WebQuests for one or more lessons in that unit.

ENGAGE, SUPPORT & DAZZLE

We have all likely experienced a lecture (or two or more) like the one featured in the iconic movie, *Ferris Bueller's Day Off*. The teacher drones on and on as the camera pans to students who are asleep, rolling their eyes and otherwise desperately waiting for the class to end. It is a funny scene, not only because of the content ("It was called Voodoo Economics"), but because of the truth it conveyed! The scene of the social studies teacher with no affect and a monotone voice became a vivid reminder of how very dull a lecture-based lesson can be.

Because of the bad rap lecture often gets from films like *Ferris Bueller* and from education researchers (Freeman et al., 2014; Mazur, 2009), some teachers may feel that using whole-class instruction is always discouraged in the differentiated classroom. This is simply not accurate. While it is true that traditional "sage on the stage" teaching should not be the centerpiece of every lesson plan, formats like whole-class discussion and lecture certainly have a place in the co-taught classroom. After all, every lesson cannot feature a scintillating simulation, professional-level project or tantalizing tableau! Therefore, on Day 20, we offer our dear readers a range of strategies for keeping traditional forms of instruction lively, engaging and comprehensible.

Show What You Know

Some students may not be able to follow a lecture without related visual supports, and most others will be more engaged and interested if there are props, notes, diagrams, photos or models that support the content. By simply scanning lesson plans and asking, "How can we show, demonstrate, or illustrate this concept or lesson?," you may come up with fresh ideas you had not previously considered. For instance, you can use unexpected objects to make key points (e.g., bring in different types of balls to show the relative sizes of the planets; use two intersecting hula hoops to create a 3-D Venn diagram). You might also use photographs as a visual support (e.g., illustrate challenging vocabulary words like *indignant*, *nefarious* and *vociferous*), create infographics with tools like www.piktochart.com and www.venngage.com or make colorful posters of useful diagrams, reminders or key questions with www.postermywall.com or www.pixteller.com.

In addition to these "show and tell" ideas, you may also need more general presentation supports to help students who profit from more than one mode of output in a lesson. Many educators use PowerPoint or other presentation software for daily lectures and whole-class lessons. These programs are ideal for busy teachers because they allow you to create lecture materials once and refine them over time as your audience changes and as the content needs to be revised. This customized content can be sent to student laptops so learners can follow along in real time. Additionally, creating hard copy note sets for students is as easy as hitting the print button on the computer, and these products can be adapted for the needs of diverse learners by changing images and colors and by varying the amount of text or information on each slide.

Want even more ideas for creating top-notch presentation visuals? Check out www.haikudeck.com, www.prezi.com, www.emaze.com and www.animoto.com for alternatives to PowerPoint that students will both enjoy seeing and trying themselves.

Keep Them Talking

Thinking out loud not only provides a bit of a brain break for restless students, but gives the teacher an opportunity to eavesdrop on conversations and informally assess what is being learned and understood.

To get and keep your students talking, you can use any number of response techniques in your classrooms. You might regularly move students into small groups so they can learn with and from one another. Or you can throw an object (e.g., beach ball, stuffed toy, bean bag) around the classroom to elicit quick responses from those who catch it.

You can also get them chatting with a game of "stand and share." Just call out a category (e.g., May birthdays, those wearing tennis shoes) and anyone fitting that category has to stand and share a response to a prompt or content-based question.

Another quick and easy way to create a little chitchat is to implement a "turn and talk" technique. At certain intervals in your lecture, ask students to turn to the person next to them (or assign partners in advance) and discuss the content just presented. To make the exercise even more purposeful, you might give students a specific prompt. For instance:

> » *Ask your partner a question about …*
> » *Provide an application for the idea we just presented.*
> » *Draw one thing we just presented and tell your partner about the illustration.*
> » *Share something we presented that was surprising/interesting/confusing.*
> » *Paraphrase what we just taught.*
> » *Define a vocabulary word we used in the first fifteen minutes of this lecture.*

Cut Them Loose

Many learners do their best work when they are moving. These are the students who often wiggle in their chairs or tap their feet while you are presenting the lesson. If you have several students like this in your classroom, you may want to create more opportunities for active learning during your lectures. "Stop the Lecture & Start the Drama" (Udvari-Solner & Kluth, 2008) is one technique teachers can use to blend lecture and movement. To engage in this humorous and easy-to-implement activity, simply assign students roles in short skits at specific points in the lesson. These sketches can be serious renditions of important facts or can be developed as parodies or satires of a situation. This activity works best to illustrate events, demonstrate roles of critical figures in history or to show a process, cycle or sequence. Props are optional but encouraged! Examples in a social studies class might be to replay moments in history like the invention of the telephone or the building of the pyramids. Examples in an elementary math class might be to have students physically demonstrate addition, subtraction or the creation of sets and subsets.

You can also give opportunities for movement by simply asking students to respond to lecture questions or statements in more active ways. For instance, students can respond to the question, "What is one half of one half?" by using:

- » *mini-chalkboards or mini-dry erase boards;*
- » *a physical response (e.g., "Walk to the front of the room if you think the answer is one-half, walk to the back of the room if you think the answer is one-fourth and stay where you are if you are not sure");*
- » *pre-made cards (e.g., all students have ½, ¼ and ⅛ flashcards on their desks and they hold one of them up in response to teacher questions);*
- » *sidewalk chalk on the playground;*
- » *window markers on desktops or windows; or*
- » *"graffiti-style" words and pictures scribbled on chart paper posted around the room or "Michelangelo-style" words and pictures scribbled on chart paper stuck to the bottom of student desks or tables.*

Delight In The Doodle

In a 2009 study published in *Applied Cognitive Psychology*, psychologist Jackie Andrade set out to explore the effect of doodling on memory. Study participants were asked to listen to a mock voicemail message from the host of an upcoming birthday party. In the message, the host skipped around to a few different topics (e.g., a redecorated kitchen) but also mentioned several places and the names of all of the party guests. Half the study participants were asked to shade in shapes on a piece of paper while they listened to the message. The other half didn't doodle at all. All of the participants were asked to write the names of those coming to the party while the recording played, so the doodlers worked on both their doodles and their lists. Afterward, the papers were removed and the forty volunteers were asked to recall the places and the names of the people coming to the party. The result? Those who doodled recalled twenty-nine percent more than the control group!

IMPLEMENTATION TIP

If your students do not seem interested in doodling or tell you that they don't know how to create visual notes, consider that they may need to see models. When you are using one teach/ one make multisensory, you will want to show students what different kinds of graphic notes look like. Show them how to create mind maps, how to brainstorm and how to design their own graphic organizers.

What can we learn from this study? One takeaway may be that, for some students, doodling is not (as some might believe) a distraction, but a useful memory-retention tool. Therefore, instead of expecting students to sit quietly and listen, it may be helpful to give them a way to respond to presentations or lectures. Taking notes is one way to do this, of course, but you may find that they tire of the same routine day after day. Variations on traditional notetaking, however, may provide just enough novelty to help students attend a lecture or discussion and retain the information presented. Allow students to take notes in pairs (one student writes down a comment and passes it to his partner, that student jots a note and passes the paper back); let them take visual or picture notes (ask students to take continuous notes or simply to stop at regular intervals to draw images of what they just heard); or give them ideas for coding their written notes (e.g., putting a question mark by points they need more information about; putting a check mark by ideas they deem most important). Or surprise them occasionally and have them take notes on surfaces that are unexpected, such as a paper tablecloths, lunch bags, paper plates or poster boards. For even more doodle-related ideas, check out Table 20.1.

TABLE 20.1

Classroom Doodling & Drawing Ideas

These ideas can be used as the centerpiece of a lesson, as a warm up, as an energizer or even as a quick assessment.

think-draw-share	Have students draw images, doodles or phrases on index cards to summarize a piece of a lecture. Then, have them turn to a partner or partners and share cards.
text maps	Textmapping is a technique popularized by educator, Dave Middlebrook (www.textmapping.org). Textmaps are essentially book chapters copied and reconstructed in a scroll format (taped end to end). To use this idea, distribute scrolls to groups of students and have each group mark up the chapter. Students should use color, words, images, pictures and symbols to identify important information in the text and to highlight relevant concepts and words.
reaction diagrams	Use this technique in lieu of traditional notes. Give students chart paper or big sheets of drawing paper and have them create a visual representation of presented material during a longer segment of instruction. The diagrams should help students connect and understand key points.
comic strip notes	When you want to encourage students to think creatively, express themselves in a different way and illustrate ideas instead of explaining them, introduce comic strip notes. Students can create strips of a mathematical function, a chapter or passage of a book, steps of a scientific process, etc.
whole-class graffiti	After reading or discussing ideas, have students take turns getting up to draw or write reactions and memorable details on the classroom white board. Students should write large enough for all to see the ideas being shared. The process continues until the board is filled. To preserve the content, be sure to take photos of the class-created graffiti at the end of the activity.
dictionary draw	Ask a student to come to the front of the room and draw a content-related word or concept. As he or she draws the word *chaos* or a pulley or an aerobic exercise, classmates shout guesses until the correct answer is provided.

TO DO LIST

. . . .

☐ Check out alternatives to PowerPoint. Choose one to try this week.

☐ Challenge yourselves to use "turn and talk" and related strategies this week.

☐ Consider one new way to get students up and moving.

☐ Create a plan to add drawing or doodling to an upcoming lesson. Scratch that. Draw or doodle a plan to add drawing or doodling to an upcoming lesson.

DAY 21

PUT IT IN WRITING

At this point, you have learned a LOT about designing great lessons as a team. You know how to share roles, you have learned several collaborative structures and you have ideas for differentiating instruction in a co-taught classroom. It's time to put it all together and develop your plans.

We realize that both of you probably already have a favorite planning method. One of you may do your best work on the back of a napkin, and the other may have a lesson plan book that is color coded, neatly organized, filled with details and spritzed with lavender water.

Neither one of you will likely want to give up the lesson planning format, system or materials that you have used in the past, and we are not necessarily saying that you should. All we ask is that you are open to some new ideas as you begin planning together, and that you consider both of your styles as you begin the process. There is no single correct way to collaboratively plan with your partner, but it is absolutely imperative that you create a system that works well for the team and for each of you as individuals.

We will do our best to help by suggesting that you find a template you both like; plan in patterns; stack, mix and match co-teaching structures within your lessons; and evaluate your planning tools throughout the year.

Find A Template

We certainly have our favorites, but we won't be recommending any one plan, template or approach for your team. We trust you to make that decision because you are practically co-teaching pros at this point. We do, however, want to get you thinking about what high-quality, effective lesson plans look like.

At the very least, you will want to create plans that clearly delineate the roles of both teachers. You will likely also want space for essentials such as lesson objectives and materials, adaptations/ modifications and even any assessment that might be used. See Figure 21.1 for a basic template that includes these features and Figure 21.2 for a sample lesson plan. This form may work for your team if you are detail-oriented and if you need some reminders about using the co-teaching structures.

Not crazy about that template? Perhaps you and your partner would appreciate a plan that is a little more visually interesting. Check out the beauty we have created for you in Figure in 21.3. This form not only has spaces to detail the roles of both teachers during every part of the lesson, but it also has unique features such as space for a "big picture" or larger message of the lesson and an area to specifically list any differentiation techniques you plan to use.

Still not seeing the perfect plan outline for you and your partner? Maybe the two of you would prefer a dynamic system that can be easily adapted. If so, try an electronic tool like commoncurriculum.com, planbookedu.com or planboardapp.com. You can also use the systems you already have in place for sharing plans with those in your school or department such as Wikispaces.com or Groups.google. com. Or if you like the flexibility of an e-tool but prefer to "kick it old school," consider this sticky note co-planning book that we found in a sixth-grade classroom (Figure 21.4). This system allowed the co-teaching team to switch roles and change activities easily, and it honored the school-sup-ply-loving personalities of the educators who created it.

FIGURE 21.1
Co-Teaching Lesson Plan: Template

LESSON _____

📖 materials _____   assessment _____

✂ adaptations _____

⇨ objectives > _____

        > _____

        > _____

time	activities/tasks	structure	teacher #1	teacher #2
		___ duet ___ 1 teach/1 float ___ 1 teach/1 multi ___ 1 teach/1 assist ___ parallel ___ station ___ other:		
		___ duet ___ 1 teach/1 float ___ 1 teach/1 multi ___ 1 teach/1 assist ___ parallel ___ station ___ other:		
		___ duet ___ 1 teach/1 float ___ 1 teach/1 multi ___ 1 teach/1 assist ___ parallel ___ station ___ other:		
		___ duet ___ 1 teach/1 float ___ 1 teach/1 multi ___ 1 teach/1 assist ___ parallel ___ station ___ other:		
		___ duet ___ 1 teach/1 float ___ 1 teach/1 multi ___ 1 teach/1 assist ___ parallel ___ station ___ other:		

FIGURE 21.2

Co-Teaching Lesson Plan: Example

LESSON *"Three Generations...": Eugenic Sterilization in America*

📖 materials   *articles, iPads, DVD*   📋 assessment *letters to the editor*

✂️ adaptations   *group work, assistive tech, varied text complexity, graphic organizer app*

➡️ objectives > *Students will explore how science was used/misused to develop public policy.*

> *Students will be able to explain the significance of the Buck vs. Bell decision.*

> *Students will understand how historical documents can help us understand past events.*

time	activities/tasks	structure	Lacy	Ed
8:00–8:10	Show a video clip of "Against Her Will: The Carrie Buck Story."	___ duet _X_ 1 teach/1 float ___ 1 teach/1 multi ___ 1 teach/1 assist ___ parallel ___ station ___ other:	Set up the segment and show the clip.	Help Owen prep for lesson (e.g., find social studies page on device).
8:10–8:35	Pass out the article "Sterilization of the Defective, Aim" to one group (Ed) & the "Buck vs. Bell" to the other (Lacy). Students partner read & annotate. Pairs should read once to get the gist of the article. Then, read again & take notes on the following questions: » How did experts determine who would be sterilized? » Why were Carrie and her mother judged to be feebleminded? » How was the assessment of these women tied to their social class, gender & level of education?	___ duet ___ 1 teach/1 float ___ 1 teach/1 multi ___ 1 teach/1 assist _X_ parallel ___ station ___ other:	Support students reading Buck vs. Bell. Help Owen adjust readability of document. Supply adapted copies to Raul & Gia.	Support students reading the article.
8:35–8:50	Bring the group back together and discuss findings.	___ duet ___ 1 teach/1 float _X_ 1 teach/1 multi ___ 1 teach/1 assist ___ parallel ___ station ___ other:	Take notes on interactive white board.	Lead discussion (focus on ?s & help them find evidence from text). Call on Owen to share first.
8:50–9:15	Have students write responses based on their learnings. Explain that they will write a letter to the Courier-Journal editor. They should write the letter from the present year, using the knowledge and information they have about how views have changed on disability and human rights.	___ duet ___ 1 teach/1 float ___ 1 teach/1 multi ___ 1 teach/1 assist ___ parallel ___ station _X_ other: 2 float/ facilitate	Remind students to reference docs. Check in with Raul & Gia. Provide them w/ graphic organizers.	Remind students to reference docs. Check in with Owen and make sure he can print from his device.

FIGURE 21.3
Visual Co-Teaching Lesson Plan Format

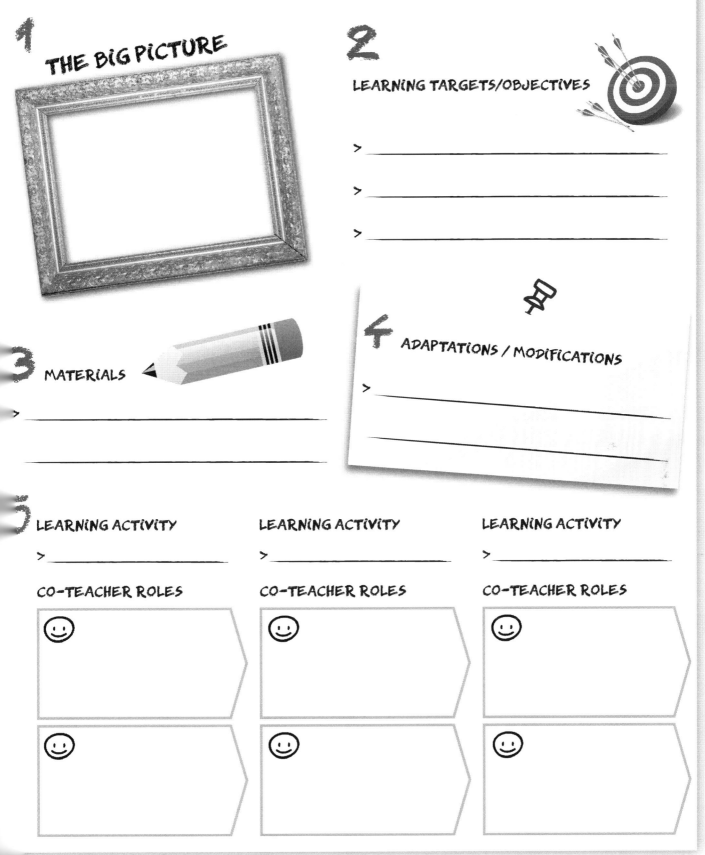

FIGURE 21.4

Sticky Note Co-Teaching Plan Book

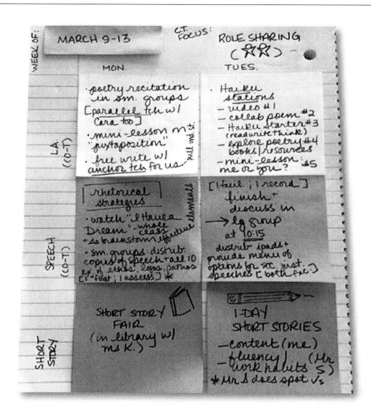

Make It Easy

Once you have your template, think creatively about how you plan. Consider all of your upcoming units and look for patterns that will make lessons more predictable and planning easier. So, if you have decided that station teaching would be a good way to introduce new material, review previously-covered content and differentiate instruction for the diverse group of students in your ninth-grade math class, consider implementing this structure on a regular basis over a period of time. You might decide to use stations every Tuesday, for instance, or to kick off every new unit of study for the next quarter.

Patterns also make collaboration easier for other professionals in the building. For instance, if you use anchor activities every other Monday morning in order to work with individual students on long-term projects, the ELL teacher or reading specialist may see this as an ideal time to support students and, therefore, may make make an extra effort to work in your classroom any time they have this time period free.

Mix & Match

Another trick to keep in mind when planning for two is to "mix and match" your co-teaching structures, not only throughout the week but within a lesson. Just because you start a lesson using one teach/one make multisensory doesn't mean you can't end that lesson with a parallel teaching structure. During some lessons, in fact, you may want to shift structures two or three or more times if this is the best way to meet the targeted lesson objectives and support your learners. Take a peek at Figure 21.2 again, and you will notice that the team teaching in this block-schedule lesson used four different structures in just seventy-five minutes.

Review & Revise

After you have been planning for a while, take stock of what is working and what needs tweaking with your system. If your plans are too detailed, talk about how to simplify. If your paper-based system is hard for two to manage, consider trying an electronic version. If you don't like the electronic system you have chosen, give yourselves permission to try another one. You will also want to analyze past plans for content. Evaluate how often you are using certain co-teaching structures. Assess how you are role sharing. Look across a week or more of plans to see how many different types of lesson formats you are using.

Keep this process going throughout the year or at least until you feel you have achieved planning perfection.

TO DO LIST

☐ Review the lesson plan suggestions in this section with your co-teaching partner.

☐ Evaluate the plans you are currently using and discuss any changes you might want to make. For instance, would you like to try an electronic planning system? Include new elements or features? Change the template you are using? Add scratch-and-sniff stickers?

☐ Achieve planning perfection.

DAY 22

TEACH THE TEACHER

After learning all of those new ways to keep learning fresh and memorable for the students in the co-taught classroom, let's remember that teachers are learners too and that we also need inspiration and motivation throughout the year. For this reason, we are going to shift gears today to focus on ideas that will help you and your co-teaching partner teach and learn from one another.

In co-teaching, when you share roles you have to share knowledge. Co-teaching partners certainly share information all day, all week and all year long about their students, but we feel they should also be sharing expertise and ideas related to teaching itself.

So, what might this teaching-the-teacher scenario look like? Let's imagine that the special education teacher knows one hundred ways to make lectures more engaging and he or she is teaming with a social studies teacher who mainly lectures. Some peer coaching here might be helpful. The special education teacher might suggest new ways to share information or model active lecturing techniques. He or she might suggest ways to "shake up" whole-class instruction with visuals, technology or a dramatic reenactment or two (think Lewis and Clark costumes, snappy dialogue and a few key points inked on a canoe-shaped poster). The social studies teacher will then need to share information about the content and support his or her partner in understanding all of the salacious details of the Corps of Discovery and Fort Clatsop.

Co-teachers need to embrace their partner's expertise and be open to being tutored by their colleagues formally and informally throughout the year. We know a team of co-teachers who asked to be dismissed from a professional development day for this purpose. One teacher taught his partner how to use assistive technology tools (e.g., Dragon Naturally Speaking, Co-Writer) that they could use to support several students in the classroom, and his partner used the time to teach his colleague about the new science standards and virtual resources they could tap into as they planned for their four shared classes. They wrote up their information-sharing plan and submitted it to their administrators. They were granted the opportunity to work together for a half of a day, and both of them left with useful skills, new knowledge and a deeper understanding and appreciation of the abilities and needs of their partners.

This process should not be a struggle. Like teaching your students, it should be fun or at least mildly diverting. To start, determine where you have expertise and where you might like to expand your own learning. Then, decide how you would like to share with and learn from your co-teaching partner.

Assessing Skills & Needs

When you start co-teaching, you have another teacher observing your work day in and day out; you are likely tackling new skills and challenges, and you may even be dealing with larger numbers of students and a wider range of needs than before. All of these things may seem to magnify your challenges and expose your weaknesses. For example, if you start spending a lot of time with the business technology teacher and you are not terribly tech-savvy, it may become immediately clear that you have to grow your skill set when you are looking around the room for the floppy discs and asking the students to help you log into the "thingy" using the "other thingy."

Co-teaching can certainly make one feel vulnerable, but keep in mind that working with a partner should also help you see your strengths more clearly. Another adult will see how gracefully you handled three consecutive classroom disruptions and how you acted out the life cycle of the butterfly with equal parts energy and drama. In the best case scenario, these moments are not only witnessed, but acknowledged and maybe even cheered.

One of the many gifts of a co-teaching relationship is that it can help you improve in areas of need and capitalize on areas of strength. In order to realize this benefit, however, you and your partner need to have a clear idea of what you are working with in terms of skills, competencies, struggles and challenges. In other words, you need to begin learning from one other by assessing what you have and what you need. To make you feel confident about the whole thing, we recommend that you begin your self-evaluation by examining strengths. Then, you can move on to needs. It always helps to start with the good stuff. Don't you agree?

Strengths

It can be hard for teachers to identify and own their strengths. Some educators may feel self-conscious about sharing their best traits and skills with others as it can feel a little "braggy" and, therefore, awkward. Others may hesitate to share because they simply are not accustomed to identifying their own abilities. In other cases, teachers may not realize some or all of the gifts they possess. We admit it. This task isn't always easy. It is, however, necessary.

Trust us. Even if you struggle to identify a list of gifts, abilities and strong points, you have many. For example, you may excel in one or more of these areas:

» *differentiating assessments*
» *working with students with challenging behavior*
» *flipping the classroom*
» *teaching food webs seven different ways*
» *threading sewing machines*
» *conducting a running record*
» *serving a volleyball*
» *creating stop-motion videos*
» *making learning multisensory*
» *reciting monologues from Hamlet*
» *creating on-the-spot visual supports*
» *playing Minecraft*
» *speaking Spanish*
» *developing rubrics*
» *conducting hair-bending science experiments*

Keep in mind that no strength is too small to mention in this process. Any skill or talent that you possess may be a potential learning opportunity for your co-teaching partner. As you can see from the list on the previous page, the items you generate can be directly connected to teaching (e.g., conducting hair-bending science experiments) or indirectly connected to teaching (e.g., playing Minecraft). Now, ready or not, take a moment and list at least ten skills, abilities or competencies connected to your life in the classroom. It's okay. Boast a bit!

> _____   > _____

> _____   > _____

> _____   > _____

> _____   > _____

> _____   > _____

Needs

Now, take a moment and identify a few of your more pressing areas of need. This list tends to be easier to build as most of us focus more on our areas of challenge than on our areas of ability. Still, some of you may struggle with this task because you are unsure of which areas to prioritize or how general or specific to be. If you do get stuck, we recommend that you consider not only your obvious challenges, but the abilities you have observed in your co-teaching partner. This way, you can identify areas of growth that are directly connected to areas of strength for someone who is in a position to teach and support you.

Your areas of need may potentially include:

- » *writing measurable goals*
- » *sticking to lesson plans*
- » *programming a student's AAC (augmentative and alternative communication) device*
- » *diagramming sentences*
- » *facilitating literature circles*
- » *keeping students awake during lessons on linear equations*
- » *changing the learning state regularly*
- » *coaching students during the circuit training unit*

- » *designing sensory supports for students on the autism spectrum*
- » *learning to use the new student blogging platform*
- » *remembering if a turtle is a reptile or an amphibian*
- » *returning pencils to a co-teacher's desk*
- » *being on time*
- » *understanding Snapchat*
- » *learning to use new e-portfolios with biology students*

Again, feel free to add items to your list that are directly connected to teaching or indirectly connected to teaching. Take a moment and list at least ten areas of need or challenge related to your life in the classroom. Be honest. We're all friends here.

> _____

> _____

> _____

> _____

> _____

> _____

> _____

> _____

> _____

> _____

Teaching, Learning & Coaching

Now that you have determined strengths and needs, think about how you might want to share your knowledge and gain needed skills and expertise. Are you at a loss? Can't think of any creative ways to get and give help? Worry not. We have several suggestions for how to begin your on-the-job, ongoing, colleague-to-colleague coaching experience.

Teach As You Teach

This idea is the easiest, and, perhaps, the most powerful. It simply involves making a commitment to watching your co-teaching partner in action and learning from their daily work.

We once observed two Kindergarten co-teachers who were so new to the job that they did not understand the full power of their tendencies to engage in teach-as-you-go learning. We observed for thirty minutes, however, and were struck almost immediately at the potential benefits of their daily in-between-lesson interactions. As the special education teacher finished engaging in a small group book chat, her co-teaching partner whispered, "I loved how you let other kids try using Troy's device during the lesson. They probably loved it." The special education teacher said, "Yeah! I always do that. Troy loves it too. It's actually one of the best ways to help students master new assistive tech. They can see what it looks like to use the device, and they get excited because they are not the only one using it." The general education teacher immediately said, "Well, I should be doing that too!" Minutes later, she was creating a thematic map with all of the students, as the special education teacher set up materials for an upcoming science project. We noticed that the special education teacher was really interested in the lesson and watched intently as her colleague created a powerful learning tool with and for her students. When students transitioned to the science activity, the special educator told us, "That is something I want to do more often. Next time we create one, I'll probably ask to lead the group."

Tiny Trainings

Peruse the "areas of need" lists of your co-teacher and of any others on your collaborative team (e.g., therapists, paraprofessionals). Look for topics on their lists that are areas of strength for you and offer to craft short talks on those topics. So, if a colleague lists "using Twitter" on her list, you might offer a twenty-minute training on the topic after school or during lunch to bring everyone up to speed on how to use social media as a communication, community-building or writing support. Another way to fuel your "tiny training" agenda is to regularly review your own needs lists and seek people out who might be able to offer the support you require. Talks might be given by anyone in your circle, including your assistant principal, student council president, a parent volunteer or school nurse.

Handy Handouts

Design or search for one-page handouts or brief articles to share with one another (e.g., 5 Key Themes in *Beowolf*; Universal Design for Learning in Art Class; Tips for Communicating with Families of English Language Learners). Keep good teaching know-how in mind when presenting the material; remember that teachers are learners too. This means choosing or creating pages that are easy to read, filled with clear examples and relevant for your audience. Toss in a few graphics, too (a bit of darling clip art never hurt anybody). Use your handouts to inspire discussion when you are meeting and planning or simply offer them as resources that can be used as references or reminders.

Coffee Klatch Catch-Up

Have a coffee with your co-teaching partner and take turns informally sharing information on topics related to your classroom, your students and your lessons. One team we know meets for coffee one Tuesday a month and takes turns sharing a new website or e-resource. These "Tech Tuesdays" serve as an excuse to socialize for a few minutes and force them both to dive into unknown techy territory that they might otherwise avoid.

To make these meetings as fruitful as possible, consider brainstorming a list of "coffee talk" topics at the beginning of the year and choosing one to chat about every time you fill your cups together. Or do it right now. Go ahead. We can wait.

Have A Barbara Walters Moment

Is there a teacher you admire for her collaboration with the occupational therapist or remarkable ability to collect and analyze data in the classroom? If so, ask if you and your co-teacher can set up a time to interview her. Sit down for ten minutes and pick her brain. You don't need to make it too formal so leave your camera crew behind. Do, however, offer to bring snacks or a great new read-aloud suggestion in return for the advice and information.

Using That Knowledge

Now that you have learned, taught and shared, it's time to show off! Don't just pat yourself on the back when you become a sign language expert or master of literacy assessments, go out and use what you now know and encourage your co-teaching partner to do the same. Look for opportunities to polish newly acquired abilities as you plan and teach lessons and make a conscious effort to keep growing new skills all year long. For many teachers, this daily professional development is one of the best aspects of co-teaching. So take advantage of it as both a teacher and a learner.

And don't forget to thank your co-teaching partner for making you look good and for contributing to your growth as an educator. You can just say, "You are the best!" or you can show your gratitude with a pumpkin spice latte. Or to really illustrate your appreciation, you can teach your professional sidekick something in return. Still get them the pumpkin spice latte, though. Everyone likes pumpkin spice latte.

TO DO LIST

- ☐ Make a list of your skills. Then, make a list of your needs. Have your partner do the same.
- ☐ Choose at least one method for teaching one another on a regular basis (e.g., tiny trainings).
- ☐ Rock your new knowledge big time.

COLLABORATE WITH THE CLASS

At this point you may be thinking, "Co-teaching is great, but I wish we had an even bigger team to meet all of the needs in our classroom." We must have read your mind, because we are about to share some ideas for enlisting the support of several new collaborative partners: your students.

Why should you and your partner be the only ones planning, presenting, explaining, exploring and facilitating? Students are capable of playing many different roles in the collaborative classroom and giving them opportunities to do so will not only help them build skills and understand content in new ways, but allow them to learn about learning itself.

So, kick back, relax and hand over that plan book, pointer and "A+ Teacher" mug. It's time to collaborate with the class.

Five Student Roles In The Co-Taught Classroom

There are dozens of ways students can work in a classroom to make the day more challenging, interesting, productive and rigorous; we will highlight our five favorite roles in this section.

Tutors

It is a wonder that tutoring relationships are not more common in both elementary and secondary schools given the positive outcomes associated with this practice. Peer tutoring puts teaching in the hands of students and provides opportunities for them to learn a host of skills including active listening, paraphrasing, clarifying, providing feedback and engaging in critical thinking.

There are several different types of tutoring to try. In peer-to-peer models, tutoring occurs between students of the same age or grade level. One learner may have more knowledge or expertise than his or her partner or—more commonly—the two students may be equal or near equal in skill or ability and may be teaching or supporting one another through the use of answer keys, tutor scripts or other support tools. In a peer-to-peer session, students usually alternate roles as tutor and tutee. Alternatively, you could engineer a peer-to-peer model so that the students' roles within a tutoring session remain the same and one primarily serves as the tutor and one as the tutee for the entire segment of time.

Cross-age tutoring is another popular support model for collaborative classrooms. Tutors may be culled from upper grades within the same school or from different buildings (e.g., high school students tutoring those in middle school). In this model, older students serve as tutors for younger tutees.

Mentors

Mentors are different from tutors in that they may not teach anything directly. Instead they typically serve as coaches or advocates for learners needing direction, inspiration or advice. A mentor is usually an older student or just one that has more experience than his or her mentee. An older child with learning disabilities or low vision might serve as a mentor for a younger child with the same needs. Or a student with a specific sort of expertise (e.g., coding, playing the cello) could mentor a peer who who shares his or her passion or interest.

Study Partners

In her book, *The Dreamkeepers*, Gloria Ladson-Billings (1994) highlights the work of a teacher who insists on cooperation and asks students to "buddy up" starting on the first day of school. She shares that she commonly talks to student buddies when learners are struggling. She reminds them that they are helpers and need to look out for their partners and it works: "Within a couple of months, I begin to see them support one another. One student will hesitate before he turns in his paper and will go check to make sure the buddy is doing okay" (p. 72).

This type of reciprocal support can teach responsibility and create a sense of cooperation and community in the classroom. If you think this idea can work with your students, assign long-term learning partners who work together to review, study and teach or switch up your partners regularly and strategically based on the difficulty, content and demands of lessons.

Resident Experts

Students with a host of skills and abilities can serve as resources for one another. This typically happens quite naturally, but you can raise the status of this role by asking students to choose which kind of resident expert they want to be. After they have made their selections, give them opportunities to share their expertise in formal and informal ways. You could have resident experts in any number of areas, including graphic design, gardening, reading and speaking Japanese.

Managers

Need yet another idea for collaboration? How about assigning students to act as classroom managers? One or more learners can contribute by taking over the business of the classroom, including keeping paperwork neat and organized, storing and charging tablets and computers, placing phone calls, Tweeting daily happenings and sending e-mails (e.g., contacting a local museum to help plan a field trip).

IMPLEMENTATION TIP

When using the role of manager, start with those students who may need to move more or who may benefit from the extra boost of confidence that can come from providing support. Be sure to rotate this role as time goes on.

How About Teaching?

It's great to have students act as tutors, mentors, study buddies, resident experts and managers, but if you really want to up your game when it comes to differentiation and collaboration, invite students to teach. You don't necessarily have to get all of your new co-teaching partners their own grade books, apple-shaped jump drives or "Teachers Change the World" inspirational quote-a-day perpetual calendars, but you should absolutely share your knowledge, expertise and enthusiasm with your new colleagues. If possible, talk to all of your students about instructional techniques throughout the year. Give brief demonstrations. Make short readings on teaching strategies available to them. And—depending on the age of your learners—be explicit about the teaching decisions you make throughout the year, and let them know why you make certain choices and how you design certain lessons.

Once students have some ideas about teaching, you can involve them in daily practice in several different ways. You can formally invite students into co-teaching by assigning individuals to deliver certain lessons on their own or with you and your co-teaching partner. You can also turn this work over to small groups of students or pairs of learners who can model co-teaching structures of their own. Or you can look for co-teaching support in more informal ways by bringing students to the front of the classroom for short mini-lessons on content they know well. Alternatively, you can bring learners forward to co-present on material they do not know well as a way to help them learn the material. In these instances, students might participate in a demonstration or co-facilitate a discussion with one or both of their teachers.

Wait! There's More

These ideas are just the tip of the iceberg that is your collaborative classroom. There are so many other roles that young people may learn from and thrive in if we design our classrooms with them as our partners. Students may serve as:

» *inspirational quote sharers*
» *fact-of-the-day finders*
» *word wizards (finds new words and/or new ways to learn words)*
» *community-building experts*

» *daily DJs*
» *dance party DJs*
» *standards secretaries (helps teachers consider ways to teach and learn the standards)*

» *classroom organizers/ designers/decorators*
» *scribes*
» *photographers*
» *documentarians*
» *history buffs*

- » current events curators
- » librarians
- » advice columnists
- » inclusion evaluators
- » mathematicians/ statisticians
- » science guys/gals

- » musicians
- » celebration chairs
- » topic experts
- » social chairs
- » treasurers
- » stress busters
- » poets

- » materials managers
- » fun makers
- » bloggers
- » Tweeters
- » Instagram curators
- » philosophers

This is only a partial list, of course. What other roles could you assign your students? If you are struggling to generate ideas, think of the unique gifts and talents of those in your classroom. Create a list of ideas here, and turn to your students for even more potential roles.

> _____

> _____

> _____

> _____

> _____

> _____

> _____

> _____

> _____

> _____

TO DO LIST

☐ Select one new collaborative role you would like your students to adopt (e.g., tutors, mentors).

☐ Plan an awe-inspiring co-teaching lesson with one or more of your students.

☐ Choose three roles from the "Wait! There's More" section and integrate them into your classroom. Don't skip this step if you are a teacher in middle or high school. Older students can absolutely take on roles from this list, often with fewer reminders and a lot less guidance than students in early grades.

PARTNER WITH PARAS

Don't panic, but we are about to throw a wrench into the works of your well-oiled co-teaching machine. At this point you are probably starting to feel confident about collaborating with one other adult. We are thrilled about that. Before you get too comfortable, however, we need to remind you that...ahem...you might actually be working with two other adults as you support diverse learners in your co-taught classroom. In fact, it's possible that some of you may be working with three or even more adults. Before you start to hyperventilate or pack your bags for Aruba, keep reading so we can let you know that partnering with more adults can mean a bit more work, but it can also mean support for students and for your co-teaching team, relief from some responsibilities and often, a lot more creativity, inspiration and fun in the classroom.

There is one slight problem with receiving this extra support. Most teachers have received little (read: no) training on how to direct the work of paraprofessionals. Therefore, this responsibility can initially be a real challenge for some educators—especially those who are also dealing with the questions, uncertainties and novelties that come with a new co-teaching situation. For these reasons, we felt this book would be woefully incomplete without paying some attention to the special needs of those who make us look good and lighten our workload. On Day 24, let's explore the role of the paraprofessional, tips for support and the challenges and benefits of working with two or more adults in the co-taught classroom.

The Role Of Paraprofessionals

Some students may need more support than even the best co-teaching team can provide. In these cases, paraprofessionals may be assigned to work in your classroom. These individuals are important members of the educational team. Even when a paraprofessional is technically assigned to assist one or a few students with disabilities, it is critical that they are viewed as a support for all and as a part of the teaching team (Giangreco, Suter & Graf, 2011). Paraprofessionals can offer assistance in many different ways. They can lead small group instruction designed by the teaching team, provide support for personal care needs of individual students, create learning materials, facilitate interactions between students and even create on-the-spot adaptations with guidance from you and your co-teaching partner.

The roles and responsibilities of the paraprofessional will vary depending on many different factors, including the needs of the students and the demands of the classroom. For this reason, it is important not only to give your paraprofessional the district handbook of general guidelines, but to outline the expectations for his or her specific position. To create the best possible atmosphere for you, your co-teaching partner and your paraprofessional, be sure to have this conversation on the first day of school and at regular intervals throughout the year.

When expectations are not clearly outlined, paraprofessionals may be pulled in different directions by those who direct and supervise them; this may be especially true in a co-taught classroom where two different professionals may serve as direct supervisors all day long. For example, if one of you asks the paraprofessional to work with Group A and the other approaches him and asks him to work with Group B, he may be confused. If this pattern is repeated several times during one lesson, he may not only lose a pound or two in all of the transitions, but feel a little frustrated. This blunder could also cause your usually-reliable team member to "forget" to bring Dunkin' Donuts coffee to your next team meeting. Horrors!

Could you use more guidance in this area? We thought so. Check out Table 24.1 for roles a paraprofessional can have and those he or she should not adopt. This list can be used as a conversation starter and can even serve as a tool for communicating with other collaborative partners who may be supervising the paraprofessionals in your classroom (e.g., building leaders).

TABLE 24.1

The Role of the Paraprofessional

Paraprofessionals can:

» lead small group and individual instruction designed by teachers

» adapt lessons under the guidance and supervision of teachers

» gather and organize classroom materials

» monitor student progress (e.g., take data)

» design classroom materials/supports under the supervision of teachers (e.g., graphic organizer, picture schedule, adapted writing journal)

» program augmentative communication devices for classroom activities and lessons

» provide assistance for personal care/physical needs

» assist students to participate in lessons (e.g., help them follow directions)

» supervise students as they engage in small-group or independent work

» facilitate interactions between students

» carry out behavior plans

» serve as the communication contact for families on issues related to a student's schedule, classroom/school happenings (e.g., upcoming projects, school dance) and general needs

Paraprofessionals cannot:

» design curriculum, instruction or assessment

» develop data collection or assessment strategies

» determine learning goals for lessons/units

» create a behavior plan or design behavior support strategies

» discuss a student's progress, program and concerns with staff members

» serve as the communication contact for families on issues of student progress, program and concerns

Paraprofessionals In The Co-Taught Classroom

Much of the content of this book can apply to partnering with paraprofessionals. You can simply read "co-teacher" and think "paraprofessional," and much of the same sage advice will apply. However, paraprofessionals are unique in some ways when it comes to levels of training, classroom roles, responsibilities and needs. Therefore, they may need supports and guidance that you would not provide to a co-teaching colleague. We recommend that teaching teams develop strategies to communicate respect for their paraprofessionals, coach them, plan with and for them, make time for them and show a little love and appreciation now and then.

Give A Little R-E-S-P-E-C-T

Show respect for your paraprofessional from day one by welcoming him or her as a partner. We have seen paraprofessionals introduced as helpers or aides as in "Ms. Marks will be Dora's helper this year," and we find that this kind of labeling is distancing for both the students and the adults. We have also seen situations where the paraprofessional is all but ignored and that is equally troubling. We realize you will want to make all students feel comfortable and that you may worry about some learners being singled out, but please avoid practices that make your paraprofessional feel invisible (e.g., "This is Ms. Marks. She will try not to bother us. Pretend she isn't here"). Instead of these less-than-desirable options, simply introduce your paraprofessional as part of your teaching team and treat him or her as such (e.g., "This is the incomparable Ms. Marks. She is another one of the educators in our room. She will be supporting you, working in the classroom and collaborating with us all year long").

You want to regularly communicate to students that all adults in the classroom are educators. Therefore, you want to be sure to share tasks that are routine and communicate authority. Any adult in the classroom can take attendance, place goggles at each lab station, lead a brain break, read announcements, post the mental math challenge, recite the poem of the day or facilitate a review game. Having all educators share basic classroom responsibilities helps to create an atmosphere where every adult is seen as a member of the teaching team.

Another element of communicating respect is attending to the issues of equity featured on Day 10. If you have already made a commitment to put both teachers' names on the classroom door, why not feature the names of all three educators? If you have already carved out equal work space for you and your co-teacher, go back and consider how to make that same space work for three. Were you already planning on dressing up as Lincoln and Washington for Presidents' Day? No problem. Get a Roosevelt costume too. In fact, get two more costumes and invite one more colleague to join in (perhaps the vision itinerant or the enrichment coordinator), and the four of you can represent Mount Rushmore. Can you think of a better way to make sure your relationships are rock solid? (See what we did there?)

Inform, Coach, Assess And Repeat

Paraprofessionals should be our partners in educating students. They should absolutely have opportunities to contribute to the development of the educational programs and instructional plans for those learners they support but should not be given sole responsibility for these activities. No matter their level of training or expertise, paraprofessionals should always be implementing programs and plans designed by their supervising teacher—that's you. In other words, you and your co-teaching partner are responsible for setting your paraprofessionals up for success. Therefore, you will have to have conversations about each student's learning, academic, social and behavioral needs. You will have to share student IEPs and talk about not only the supports in place, but the reason for choosing and using those particular supports.

Once paraprofessionals are on the job, keep information coming in the form of coaching. Use a range of strategies to teach and support your paraprofessionals. Let them observe as you and your co-teacher work with students. Observe them as they engage in new activities (e.g., facilitating peer tutoring, implementing a new feeding program). Assess their work and provide them with feedback (e.g., "Before you present the array of choices, be sure he scans the communication menu"; "Try cueing him to ask a peer for help before he seeks help from you").

Provide A Plan

In a classroom we visited, a paraprofessional made decisions related to one student's curriculum and instruction all day long. The general educator in this classroom told us that the child, who had multiple disabilities, was included in lessons only when the paraprofessional decided the activity would benefit him. The paraprofessional didn't necessarily want this responsibility, but her supervising teachers had not given her much direction beyond, "Use your best judgment." This system of decision-making is problematic on many levels, but one of the most egregious mistakes made by this team was failing to plan and provide clear guidance. A paraprofessional should never be in the position to make such significant decisions regarding a student's education. Although many paraprofessionals are incredibly competent and skilled (some are even certified educators), it is always the teachers' professional and legal responsibility to plan curriculum and instruction and engineer a student's participation in daily lessons.

Discuss and clarify the roles and responsibilities of both the teacher and the paraprofessional either when you begin your work or after reading this book. For instructional segments, provide written directions like those provided in the sample plan in Table 24.2. This type of plan should be used consistently and updated as needed.

TABLE 24.2
Paraprofessional Lesson Plan: Example

Morning Meeting: Week of September 6–10

activity	supports needed
read-aloud	On Monday & Tuesday, please draw out the story as I read (using the scroll paper); this will be helpful as we transition into having students draw a retelling. If Dominic needs direct support, Jen or I can take over the drawing task. On Wednesday, we will split into three small groups. We will each work with groups of 5 to read the book (*Fletcher and the Falling Leaves*); this will give Dominic, Zia and others more time to interact/ask questions. If time permits, have students act out the book in three scenes. On Thursday & Friday, Jen and I can do the read-aloud on our own. If Dominic, Amy and Zia do not need any direct support, please keep working on the learning center cue cards for Dominic (all materials for this project can be found in the green bin).
calendar	Distribute the magnetic calendars to Amy, Zia and Dominic. Encourage them to sit near supportive peers. Go back to the kidney table and take observational data on the engagement & independence of Amy & Zia (forms are on Google Docs). Be sure to observe students for 8-10 minutes. At the end of calendar, get Dominic's device ready to go. He will be the first to ask and answer a question during Q & A this week.
Q & A	Cue Dominic to ask his question, if needed. If he seems to struggle, stay with the group. If he does not need direct support, please set up the tables for writing workshop including Dominic's slant board and writing box. If time permits, get the iPads set up for Amy and Zia too.

Make Time

Because they are such central members of the collaborative team, paraprofessionals must be given ample opportunities to learn new skills, voice concerns, ask questions and share ideas. If they cannot be included in regular team meetings due to time or scheduling constraints, then other tools and structures for communicating and sharing must be designed and implemented.

It is unlikely that the administrative team at your school will assign you time to collaborate and meet with paraprofessionals. However, your success as a teaching team depends on having adequate time to talk through issues and plan together. Therefore, be sure to carve out time in your schedule to meet and communicate with paraprofessionals regularly to discuss student-specific concerns, questions and any changes in roles and responsibilities. Some teams get together for fifteen or twenty minutes before or after school on certain days. Others share lunch on occasion. For issues that do not require discussion, educators might even engage in mini-meetings during the school day. This is not usually an option when only one teacher and one paraprofessional are in the room, but in a co-taught setting, it may occasionally be possible for one teacher to present a lesson or facilitate an activity while another teacher and a paraprofessional take ten minutes to discuss and design a visual support for a few students with learning disabilities or have a short chat in the hallway about behavior supports.

IMPLEMENTATION TIP

Don't forget all you learned on Day 8 and Day 9 about holding effective and efficient meetings when you sit down to plan with paraprofessionals.

Show Some Love

Paraprofessionals can be extremely valuable assets to a team, but they may not always realize how important their contributions are to their colleagues and to the classroom. Research suggests that paraprofessionals often do not receive enough validation, appreciation and feedback about their work (Giangreco, Edelman & Broer, 2001). They may even feel like third wheels in a co-teaching situation if you and your partner don't create supports and develop strategies to include them in planning, running the classroom and engaging in daily instruction. So, remember to keep your paraprofessional involved in the life of the classroom and connected to the teaching team. This goes for all aspects of your collaborative life. For instance, if you and

your co-teacher get matching tattoos, don't ask your paraprofessional to drive you there and then leave her in the lobby paging through *Inked* magazine. Bring her back into the studio and have her roll up her sleeve and join in the fun. Well, unless she is screaming something like, "I don't want a tattoo!"

And don't forget to show your appreciation directly. It probably goes without mentioning that colleagues always appreciate a sincere "thank you" for feats big and small. So, be sure to express how grateful you are when your paraprofessional cleans up the remains of your churn-your-own-butter demonstration (while wearing an old-timey skirt and bonnet no less) during "Colonial Day" festivities or when she quickly and quietly calms a student who is struggling with an unexpected transition. You get the picture. What we are trying to say is gratitude is important and there are countless ways to express it. Need ideas? Take a peek at Table 24.3.

TABLE 24.3

Ways to Thank, Support and Honor a Paraprofessional

» Treat him or her to a meal at a breakfast or lunch meeting.

» Give cards or notes with specific messages of appreciation.

» Give him or her a professional book related to work/interests.

» Relieve him or her of duties for thirty minutes or more to allow for engagement in a professional learning opportunity (e.g., watching a video, reading an article).

» Occasionally share tasks that are challenging or unpleasant (e.g., take over a morning recess duty when the temperature drops into single digits).

» Write a small article about him or her in the school newspaper, newsletter, website or blog.

» Say, "thank you"; offer positive comments.

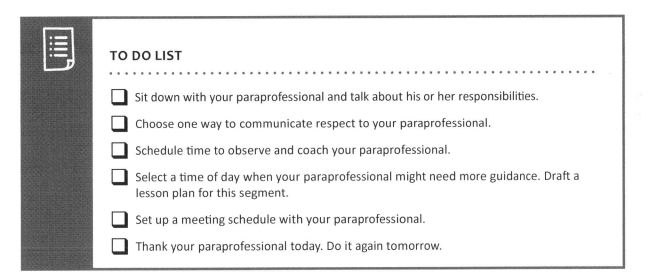

TO DO LIST

☐ Sit down with your paraprofessional and talk about his or her responsibilities.

☐ Choose one way to communicate respect to your paraprofessional.

☐ Schedule time to observe and coach your paraprofessional.

☐ Select a time of day when your paraprofessional might need more guidance. Draft a lesson plan for this segment.

☐ Set up a meeting schedule with your paraprofessional.

☐ Thank your paraprofessional today. Do it again tomorrow.

DAY 25

WORK IT OUT

Have you arrived at Day 25 problem-free? If so, consider yourselves lucky and incredibly unique. Very few teams are without troubles, but this is not necessarily bad news. Problems are normal and, perhaps, even helpful as they can move thinking forward and keep team members flexible and creative in their daily work.

The struggle for many teams, then, is not that they have problems, but that they operate without an articulated approach to problem solving. When problems emerge (e.g., you are neglecting to plan as often as you should, you have different views on how to support a particular student), it is important to resist wallowing or blaming. Well, on second thought, we know how hard teachers work, so maybe wallow long enough to devour a bag of barbeque potato chips under your desks. When you are done with the wallowing, however, it is critical that both of you wipe those delicious orange crumbs off your fingers, crawl back up into your chairs and kick into problem-solving mode.

To help you address any number of difficulties you may encounter this year, we are going to outline four different techniques that can be used to tackle troubles and solve classroom or interpersonal problems: Fifteen-Minute Problem Solving, SODA, Reframing and WWMCTPD. As you read, consider how each might be used to solve a problem you are currently experiencing.

Fifteen-Minute Problem Solving Process

The purpose of this exercise is to move past complaints, inspire creativity and encourage new ways of seeing struggles and designing solutions. Therefore, you will want to follow the guidelines exactly to avoid discussions that pull you into familiar ruts, such as admiring the problem or assigning blame.

To engage in a fifteen-minute problem solving session, gather your laptops, some paper and a timer. Then, move through the steps of the process listed in Table 25.1. Set your timer for the number of minutes shown in the left-hand column and follow the directions in the corresponding right-hand column. When the timer goes off, move on to the next step and set of directions.

TABLE 25.1

Fifteen-Minute Problem-Solving Process

1 minute	Have all participants describe the problem in writing. This should be done silently and individually.
1 minute	Discuss your responses.
2 minutes	Have participants rewrite the problem as a solvable question: • How might we…? • In what ways can we…? • What is one idea for…? Again, this should be done silently and individually.
1 minute	Discuss and agree on the question to answer.
4 minutes	Working silently and individually once more, have participants brainstorm to answer the selected question. Generate as many ideas as possible. These are only ideas so responses can be silly, far-fetched and even ridiculous. Don't judge the ideas at this stage.
2 minutes	Read your lists aloud.
1 minute	Highlight the most popular ideas.
1 minute	Choose the best solution. Then, determine a plan of action.
1 minute	Decide how and when you will assess the effectiveness of the solution.
1 minute	Congratulate yourselves on a job well done.

SODA

The SODA approach (Roosa, 1973) is popular in the field of education (Lamke, Pratt & Graeve, 2009; Schwarz & Kluth, 2007) and is often used for problems both large and small. The strategy can be fairly quick and easy to use and, therefore, can be used with students and teachers alike. It is similar to fifteen-minute problem solving, but there are no time limits on the phases of process. To use SODA, just follow the steps outlined in Table 25.2, and repeat when necessary.

TABLE 25.2
SODA Problem-Solving Approach

SITUATION	Clearly define the problem.
OPTIONS	Generate a wide range of possible solutions. There should be no judgment in this brainstorming phase. All possible solutions should be listed at this point.
DECISION	Look at the advantages and disadvantages for each option suggested. Choose an option to try first, but keep the list in case the first choice does not work.
ASSESS	Decide on a process or tool to assess progress and success.

Reframing

Reframing is a fairly straightforward strategy that involves exploring a problem from a new angle. The best way to engage in this process is to approach your problem by changing your question. This is a technique that we once used during a meeting on student attendance. We started by asking the group to brainstorm strategies that could be used to reduce absenteeism. A few ideas were offered, but these were fairly predictable such as, "Have the social workers make calls to families." Then, we shifted the question to, "How can we make our attendance rate soar?" This question was met with laughter and even some eye rolling, but it prompted a great discussion. Answers included:

- » *Offer prizes/drawings each week.*
- » *Have morning dance parties on the blacktop.*
- » *Talk to individual students about problems that prevent them from getting to school.*
- » *Make a ridiculous music video about the importance of consistent attendance. Share it with families.*
- » *Offer a wider range of extracurricular activities and include options students suggest.*

> » *Offer surprises! Schedule a lot of guest speakers. Have concerts in the cafeteria. Pass out healthy snacks for everyday celebrations.*
> » *Give students time to work on "passion projects" each week.*

You and your co-teaching partner can use this same approach as you run into problems in your practice. For instance, if you are focusing too much energy on trying to increase Aaron's "on-task" behavior, you might fail to consider if the task is worthwhile, motivating or appropriate. However, if you define the problem by asking, "How can we make lessons irresistible to Aaron?," you will be sure to consider that angle and many others.

WWMCTPD [What Would My Co-Teaching Partner Do]?

Is your co-teaching partner really skilled when it comes to fielding parent questions and concerns, or does he or she know just how to diffuse tense situations in the classroom? If so, use him or her as your inspiration as you work through those types of situations.

We call this WWMCTPD or the "What Would My Co-Teaching Partner Do?" technique. It simply involves taking the perspective of another person—in this case, your co-teacher—in order to generate new ideas or give you confidence in trying a new approach (Tamm & Luyet, 2004). This switch in viewpoint can be powerful, especially if you think very differently from others on your collaborative team.

If you want to formalize this strategy, you can do more than imagine your partner's response, you can ask for it. This idea works best when you both ask for and offer support at the same time. Start by writing advice-column-type notes to one another. Take no more than ten minutes to jot down your struggles. For example:

Dear Trudy,

I have noticed that Van seems to wander during fifth-period English class. I have done everything I can think of besides bribing him with a puppy. I think he is still listening, as he does well on his daily checks and assessments. I am worried, however, about the disruption to the other students. Please help.

Running Out of Ideas in Room 302

After you have each written questions, exchange problems to solve. Follow these simple guidelines as you work:

1. *Do not stop and talk about the problem.*

2. *Do not stop to empathize (e.g., "I know! I have also considered bribery!").*

3. *Do keep in mind that your only job is to share as many viable solutions as you can in the time allotted.*

This part of the process should also take about ten minutes. You can write your response in a letter or simply compile a list of ideas. When you are finished, return the question and potential solutions to your co-teacher.

Drawing on your co-teacher's advice will likely add new energy to the problem-solving process. If you need help remembering this, get yourself a little rubber bracelet and stamp it with WWMCTPD. You will not only be the envy of your school and social circle, but you will be way ahead of a fashion trend that is potentially more timeless and memorable than the one that inspired you to buy those tiger-print parachute pants circa 1984.

TO DO LIST

☐ Identify a problem to solve.

☐ Select a problem-solving method to try.

☐ Reflect on the process. Was it helpful? Might another method work better?

☐ Pat yourselves on the back. This work is necessary, but not easy. Well done.

☐ If the process was loads of fun, find another problem and solve away.

DAY 26

CHECK YOURSELVES

So, how are you doing? Well, not you personally (although we do hope all is well in your world outside of the classroom), but how are you doing in your collaborative relationship? One of the steps routinely left out of co-teaching training and implementation is assessment and review of the partnership. We want to encourage you not only to include this piece of the process in your work, but to embrace it with a big bear hug; it is such a critical component of your long-term success. After all, you wouldn't teach students all year long and fail to observe, test, quiz or otherwise evaluate them, would you? Of course not! At some point you would find it futile to continue providing instruction without having information about student knowledge, skill level, successes and struggles.

In today's educational climate, some stakeholders may see standardized tests as the best way to assess the effectiveness of a co-teaching relationship. While we feel that these instruments can be helpful in painting a partial picture of what is happening in a classroom, we don't think it is wise to use them as the only indicator of co-teaching success or failure. This is especially true in inclusive classrooms where certain students with disabilities may struggle mightily with the testing process itself and others may make remarkable progress, but at a rate that would not necessarily be reflected on formal assessments.

Another reason to assess beyond the test is to get a clearer picture of your progress as a teaching team. Standardized tests won't help you evaluate the productivity or growth of your co-teaching partnership. They may suggest how effective some of your teaching techniques are, but they won't provide insights into the health of your union or reveal how enthusiastically you and your partner have shared new roles.

For these reasons, we encourage co-teaching teams to use a wide range of methods, instruments and tools to evaluate their work. To make sure you take our encouragement seriously, we are dedicating all of Day 26 to this process.

Conduct A Review

At this point, it is likely too soon to gather a lot of data on your practice, but you can certainly "take the pulse" of your collaborative efforts and start the process of regular reviews. During these sessions, you will want to look at the goals you set on Day 3 and share any data, information or reflections you have related to them. You will also want to assess other aspects of classroom life. For example, you might discuss your successes so far and try to identify which aspects of your practice have contributed to those successes. Or you may want to talk about any problem areas and consider making adjustments to your teaching, your lessons or to the classroom itself.

Set New Targets & Assessments

In addition to regular reviews of your team goals, you may want to create new evaluation tools and targets that will provide useful information about your work as a team and about your impact on students. For instance, if you want to learn more about the effectiveness of your team meetings, you might take some time to review your meeting minutes and determine how well you are doing at following your agenda, taking helpful notes and following through on assigned tasks. Or if you want to learn a new teaching skill (e.g., segmenting longer lessons into manageable chunks; giving more think time; providing cues to individual students), you might ask your co-teaching partner to conduct a series of observations focused on that skill. Other ways you can "check yourselves" in the co-taught classroom include the following:

» *Use curriculum-based assessments and other measures that can document the amount of educational progress students are making in co-taught classes.*

» *Look at student IEPs and related data to see if your current practices and supports seem to be effective.*

» *Use regular video recording to track progress on a target area of growth. You might get footage every month of students engaging in morning meeting to assess whether or not they are becoming better at leading meetings, coming up with solutions and participating; or you could regularly record your silent reading segment and evaluate if students are improving with skills like staying on task and finding appropriate material. You could even use video to assess your teaming skills. You might, for instance, record portions of your team meetings over time to observe the changes in skills related to management and productivity.*

» *Interview colleagues and get their impressions of your work as a team; find people who will provide both encouragement and constructive criticism.*

» *Talk to families. Ask parents to give you formal or informal feedback in the form of e-mail messages, an electronic survey or interviews.*

» *Bring students into a focus group and ask a variety of questions about your work (e.g., What is working? What changes would they like to see? What parts of the day or period are working for them? What parts of the day or period would they like to see improved?).*

» *Examine any checklists or charts you are maintaining. You might track how often you make "good news" calls home to families, conference individually with students or co-teach lessons with building therapists.*

Keep in mind that assessing your partnership from multiple angles can be a tool for motivation. On those days when students do not seem to be responding positively to your efforts, reflect on the comments that you are getting from families. Or on the days when you see that two students with disabilities are not demonstrating growth on certain assessments, look to your IEP data to evaluate progress that you may be making there.

And what if you evaluate and don't get the data, evaluations and test scores you had hoped to see? Use that information as a tool for creating changes and setting new goals. This process should be ongoing in any classroom, but in a co-taught classroom, you have an advantage—you have a partner. So, while one of you is assessing the team's progress, the other can already be trying a new strategy, method or tool. No longer must you reflect, evaluate and revise alone. Sigh…isn't co-teaching grand?

TO DO LIST

☐ Identify dates and times to evaluate progress.

☐ Decide how you will measure your progress daily, monthly and annually.

☐ Review our list of ideas for checking your progress on page 213. Use any three of these to evaluate your partnership and your classroom success.

☐ Making better-than-expected progress? Do the moonwalk, pump your fists or jointly pretend to drop a microphone.

TEACH TO LEARN

Now that you have been at this for a few weeks, you are certainly still learning, but you may also be ready to share some of what you know with others. Okay, okay, we know what you are thinking, "Teach others? How can I teach others when I just started doing this work myself? I scarcely know a parity signal from a station teaching model!"

We understand that all of this still seems new to you, but we feel that one of the very best ways to learn something is to teach it to someone else. Couple that with the fact that most schools need teaching teams to learn from one another. After all, professional development money is tight in most districts, and strong co-teaching models depend upon ongoing learning and support.

At this point in the process, you have undoubtedly picked up a few tricks about collaboration and co-teaching. You have also had to learn new content, strategies and techniques related to curriculum and instruction. If you are teaching in a building with other co-teaching teams, it might be time to start trading ideas across classrooms and seeking formal and informal ways to problem-solve difficulties and inspire one other. If you are not in a building with other co-teachers, you may want to start brainstorming ways to make connections with teams in your district or community. On Day

27, we are committed to helping you with this outreach and are, therefore, outlining four ideas for sharing what you know as a tool for growth and improvement. Specifically, we will explore how to tell your story, welcome visitors, write all about it and get ready for your close-up.

Tell Your Story

If you want your co-teaching model to thrive, look for ways to tell your story. Design a short workshop that could be offered after school, talk to your school board about your experiences or simply offer to share at a faculty meeting in your building. There are so many ways story sharing can be useful. For starters, planning your session can help you and your co-teaching partner focus on what you have learned. Then, as you give the talk and field questions, you will both have opportunities to reflect on your work together. Finally, telling your story provides the opportunity to elicit suggestions from colleagues, which is so often useful in the early stages of collaborative teaming.

Not so sure you are ready for a big audience? Telling your story does not have to be a formal affair or even involve a sit-down, face-to-face gathering. One elementary school team reviewed their meeting minutes and simply wrote an e-mail to their principal to share their experiences:

> *Dear Ms. George,*
>
> *We have been reviewing our progress as co-teachers this year, and we are feeling proud of several accomplishments. We simply wanted to share this good news with you. So far, in only three weeks we have (a) designed stations that we now use regularly in ELA and in math, (b) differentiated our science unit on forces and interactions, (c) carved out a meeting time with our paraprofessional and a common planning time for the two of us, (d) started using a new meeting minutes format that is really keeping us organized and inspired, and (e) tried two new problem-solving strategies and came up with some interesting supports for a student with challenging behaviors. We are excited to let you know that we are working hard and finding a lot of success in our new team. Thank you for this opportunity to collaborate!*
>
> *The Room 212 Team*

Welcome Visitors

Many teachers get flustered when asked to open their door to visitors. Some feel self-conscious about being observed or skeptical that their work can inspire others. Others may be reluctant because they don't understand how a visit can positively influence their own work.

We find, however, that this practice is typically informative and energizing. When teachers are observed and interviewed by visitors, they tend to gain clarity about their philosophies and practices. Further, visits provide co-teachers with opportunities to talk about one another in front of one another. This can be an incredibly satisfying experience as there are far too few opportunities to share the positive aspects of co-teaching, and it can feel awkward to simply approach your partner and confess, "I love learning new vocabulary-building strategies from you!" Sharing this information in a post-observation discussion, however, can help visitors understand more about co-teaching and give your partner a boost at the same time.

Conversations with guests can actually be helpful in many ways. They can serve as opportunities to thank a colleague, reinforce what is going well or identify anything that needs improvement. For instance, if one partner feels like they have yet to make a real contribution in lesson planning, sharing this in a meeting with observers can be a non-threatening way to apologize ("I had a horrible first few weeks and resisted having a partner at first...I was actually unprofessional") or to express hopes and ideas ("Now I really enjoy co-teaching. Most of the planning has fallen to Todd so far, but I am looking forward to doing more co-planning in our upcoming unit on genetics since this is a topic where I have some knowledge").

Write All About It

We know so many savvy and creative educators who feel that nobody will care about their advice or experiences because they are "only" teachers. This is far from the truth, and we actually find quite the opposite to be true. New co-teachers often crave information from the real experts who have "been there, done that." So, if you want to help a colleague while also refining your own practice, consider putting pen to paper and sharing what you know.

Blog, create a newsletter or compose a longer article for publication. No matter what you do or how you do it, you will find that writing about your practice will move you forward in your work. Most teachers choose topics related to areas of great success in their work. For instance, one of us (Paula) once wrote an article on challenging institutional barriers to create a co-teaching model (Kluth & Straut, 2003). Paula and a co-teaching partner developed a collaborative model at a university and had to propose changes in scheduling, language and curriculum in order to pull off a joint teaching experience. They wrote about this primarily to share it with other faculty members who might find the experience useful, but they also hoped that it could function as a tool for communication with their own administrators. Having their rationale, methods and even their struggles in print invited other people at the school into a conversation and helped to make a case for co-teaching in their department in subsequent years. Writing helped to build a succinct case for collaborative work while also giving two educators opportunities to informally assess their practice. We think those are pretty impressive outcomes for such a relatively small investment in time and energy.

We hope that we are convincing you of the many benefits of writing about your work, but just in case you are not sold, we want to remind our readers that any aspect of collaborative work in the classroom may be worth putting on paper. That is, don't feel that you have nothing to write about if you are hitting more bumps than grooves in your collaborative journey. When deciding to write as a tool for improving your practice, it can be particularly impactful to choose an area of focus that you have not mastered or even one that causes you frustration. In this way, the blog post or article can serve as an invitation for problem solving. Can't find time to plan? Write a short piece about what you have learned from planning "on the fly," what you have managed to accomplish despite this hurdle and a few musings on how you are working to find more time. Then invite readers to comment or send suggestions.

Get Ready For Your Close-Up

We know the power of capturing co-teaching on film so we often encourage teams to assemble a hair and makeup team, find their best sides and get ready to use video as a way to teach and learn. Often, however, the teachers we support report that they are camera shy. For them, even being observed feels odd so these educators are likely very reluctant to be recorded on video for the purposes of professional development.

This resistance is oftentimes frustrating for administrators because great co-teaching moments caught on video can be used as tools for reflection, teaching and learning. For example, video scenes can be used to evaluate progress and practices. If you are unsure as a team if you are sharing roles and responsibilities when duet teaching, you can capture a lesson, watch the clip and evaluate your language, your mannerisms, where you position yourself in the room and even the amount of time each one of you leads instruction.

Video can also be used to encourage others to learn new co-teaching techniques. If one pair in your building has been co-teaching longer than others, ask them to film lessons highlighting several co-teaching models (e.g., parallel teaching, one teach/one make multisensory) and share these with all teams in the building. This practice will help all teachers build skills, and ensure that you all share a common language. Further, creating video for others is an ideal way to improve one's own practice. We find that teams usually engage in careful planning before recording for their peers and, when they shoot, they often "teach to impress." This motivation to dazzle on camera can result in positive and even unexpected outcomes. When we helped one co-teaching team design a station teaching lesson to be filmed, we recommended that they use large visual supports to make the lesson more comprehensible for anyone viewing the clip. We felt it would be easier for anyone watching to understand how students rotated at timed intervals if we placed a large visual timer at the front of the room. We also created big cardboard number signs for the stations and cut out huge red arrows to stick on the walls to help those watching the clip better understand the transition sequence. After shooting the lesson and watching it back, we found that although the visuals really helped to make the video more clear and informative, they also seemed to improve the lesson itself. Transitions were smoother than they had been in the past, and students asked fewer questions about the station teaching process. The teachers, therefore, used these visuals in subsequent lessons—even in those instances when their hard work would not appear on the silver screen.

Finally, video can be used to create a culture of co-teaching in your school or district. Footage of co-teaching structures, differentiated lessons, collaborative assessments and even team meetings can be captured and subsequently shared not just with fellow teachers, but with parents, school board members and community partners. It may be hard for some groups to get behind your work if they don't understand what co-teaching entails. For some stakeholders, telling is good, but showing is better.

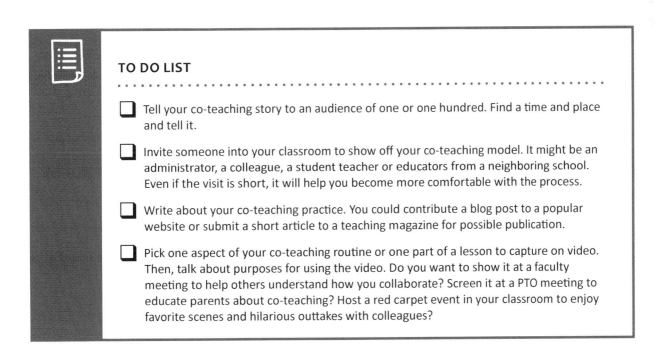

TO DO LIST

- ☐ Tell your co-teaching story to an audience of one or one hundred. Find a time and place and tell it.

- ☐ Invite someone into your classroom to show off your co-teaching model. It might be an administrator, a colleague, a student teacher or educators from a neighboring school. Even if the visit is short, it will help you become more comfortable with the process.

- ☐ Write about your co-teaching practice. You could contribute a blog post to a popular website or submit a short article to a teaching magazine for possible publication.

- ☐ Pick one aspect of your co-teaching routine or one part of a lesson to capture on video. Then, talk about purposes for using the video. Do you want to show it at a faculty meeting to help others understand how you collaborate? Screen it at a PTO meeting to educate parents about co-teaching? Host a red carpet event in your classroom to enjoy favorite scenes and hilarious outtakes with colleagues?

BUST THAT RUT

By Day 28, you will likely have mastered every element of co-teaching and won't need to hear much from us anymore... unless you get in a rut or two as the days go by. It happens to all of us. We get overwhelmed with lesson plans, triennial evaluations, report cards and committee work. Even keeping up with those Kardashians can seem exhausting after a while. The good news for co-teachers is that two educators are seldom in a rut at the same time. So, in this model, you have someone to help you climb out of that divot.

While you may already have your own strategies for getting out of a rut, we want to offer a few ourselves since you bought the book and all, and it seems the least we can do. We invite you to seek balance, learn something new, break out of your routine and make it official.

Seek Balance

Yes, co-teaching is tons of fun, good for students and probably recommended by four out of five dentists, but it isn't your life. You may need some balance if work feels like...well...work. Use your co-teaching partner to help you find professional equilibrium. Push one another to go home at a reasonable hour; you can practice your north versus south, brother versus brother, co-teacher versus co-teacher Gettysburg reenactment tomorrow during planning time. Remind one another to keep commitments under control; neither one of you needs to be the yearbook advisor, softball coach, planner of the class trip to the state capital, union representative and the chair of the "Enchantment Under the Sea" dance all in one semester.

Learn Something New

Become an expert in some aspect of your job if you are under-challenged and in a rut. Do this by getting connected to a virtual learning community, reading any number of journals or books written for educators or signing up to do a course in a related field or in your own field. Today, there are countless professional development offerings available long distance or online. If you don't have time for a whole class, just shop for bite-sized learning opportunities. Sometimes even the right sixty-minute webinar can provide the boost you need to get back in that co-teaching saddle.

Break Out Of Your Routine

Are one or both of you dragging in daily lessons? Have your props flopped? Have your visuals lost their sizzle? If so, it's time to do something new for both your students and yourselves. Try one of these tried and true recommendations for breaking out of your co-teaching routine. We swear on our collection of rubber chickens that they work.

Pick A Theme

Plan a superhero day, a backwards day (e.g., teach lessons in reverse, teach from the back of the room); a content-related day (e.g., love-a-Latin-root day, magnet appreciation day, hooray-for-Haiku day, better-know-a-biome day, celebrate symmetry day) or even a co-teaching appreciation day where you contribute the decorations and the snacks and students provide the applause and the speeches of gratitude.

Don Costumes

Work as a team to come up with thought-provoking ways to use your wardrobe as a tool and as a pick-me-up. How about showing up dressed as one another? Or coordinate outfits to match one of your units; you might choose to come as metaphor and simile, prey and predator, slope and intercept or even conductor and insulator. We once saw English teachers dressed up as a colon and semicolon; if that look can be pulled off with style and confidence, we are pretty sure any costume you can imagine can be a potential hit with students as well as an effective rut-buster.

Not really up for trying a head-to-toe look? Bring some simple accessories into your lessons. Wear matching mustaches and play a game where you quiz the students and start each question with, "We mustache you." Stroke the mustaches for maximum effect. Invest in mullet wigs and wear them during brainstorming. Tell students it is time to "mullet over." Or collect a bunch of hats and have different characters "visit" your lessons each day. Don checkered wool deerstalkers and come as Sherlock Holmes and Watson to help students form hypotheses. Have your co-teaching partner wear red horns during certain hot discussions so that he or she can play "devil's advocate" as you model a respectful debate. Get some leather flying helmets and have the Wright brothers introduce the topic of inventions.

Gather Props & Toys

Introduce new materials to liven up the classroom. Have your co-teacher march around with a huge cardboard key as you emphasize "key points" in your lecture. When your partner leads a review session, throw rubber chickens around the classroom (when students catch the chicken, they have to answer a question). Or introduce a karaoke machine during certain lessons; while one of you lectures, the other emphasizes important terms or concepts with short sing-alongs (e.g., "I got ninety-nine problems but none with multiple polynomials").

One group of teachers we observed had a habit of looking for outrageous items (e.g., purple confetti, kitchen mitts, bunny-ear headbands, fluorescent yardsticks, magic wands) in the local dollar store and seeking ways to integrate the objects into their lessons. After all, why just ask students, "Penny for your thoughts?" when you can throw an enormous coin at them and reinforce the question with a ridiculous prop?

Expand The Team

Are you really out of it? Expand your co-teaching team by getting a class pet and using it as your mascot. Have him or her create a new ritual for you. For instance, your critter could start every day with a note to the group (e.g., "Dear Class, I am embarrassed to admit it, but I have no idea what a mammal is! Can anyone help me? Love, Mr. Sniffy") This pet could also pass messages to your co-teacher during tense or awkward moments (e.g., "Mr. Sniffy, Can you tell Mr. Johnson that it is his turn to fill the Tootsie Roll bowl?").

Create New Rituals

How about changing up your daily routines and rituals as a way to energize? One idea is to start the day in a new way. You could both meet students at the door and formally greet them all as they enter the classroom, perhaps even changing up your greetings from day-to-day by bidding them a "good day" on Monday and a "top of the morning" on Tuesday. Or you could end the day in a new way, perhaps with a poem, a joke, a motivating quotation or even a whole-class selfie.

Maybe you could try some new transition cues. You know you need them if your co-teacher has flicked the lights on and off so many times the students no longer notice and, in fact, think it's cool that the classroom has a strobe light. Get out of that rut by infusing new style into those between-activity moments. Crank up Bob Marley's "Get Up, Stand Up" to cue students to come back to a whole-class format at the end of a parallel teaching lesson. Or use call and response chants to gain the attention of your students during group work. For example, when your co-teacher calls out, "Chicka chicka boom boom," you and the students respond with, "Everybody in the room" or try "Ready to rock?" followed by "Ready to roll!" (check out Table 28.1 for more ideas). By freshening up your transitions with interesting rhymes, movements and music (c'mon, why not bring out that tambourine you've tucked away for the day you get your big break as a back-up singer?), you and your co-teacher can cut down on precious transition time while bringing a bit of pizazz to the classroom.

TABLE 28.1
Call & Response Transitions for Two

Using a call-and-response-style transition can be especially effective if there are two of you to model the strategy. Try these cheers to add a little spirit to your co-taught classroom.

Teacher 1	Teacher 2 (along with class)
"What Do We Want?"	"Math"
"When Do We Want It?"	"Now!"
"Tootsie Roll"	"Lollipop"
"We've Been Talking"	"Now We Stop."
"All Set?"	"You Bet!"
"I Say 'Acids', You Say 'Bases'"	
"Acids"	"Bases"
"Acids"	"Bases"
"Hocus Pocus"	"Stop and Focus."
"That's The Way...Uh Huh Uh Huh..."	"I Like It...Uh Huh Uh Huh!"
"Na Na Naaa Na, Heyy Heyyy Hey"	"Goo-ood Job!"
"L-I-S"	"T-E-N"
"Zippity Do Da"	"Zippity A"

Make It Official

Not convinced? Tried all of the rut-busters with little success? Well, maybe the rut you are in can't be busted with devil horns, critters and tambourines alone. Maybe the only way out for you is taking your relationship to the next level. Some teams find they have accomplished all they can as mere co-teaching partners and need to make their union more official. Lucky for you, we have assembled a few impressive ideas to help you do just that.

Get Married

Many experts in the area of collaboration have likened co-teaching to marriage (Giangreco, 2007; Howard & Potts, 2009; Kohler-Evans, 2006; Murawski, 2009; Sapon-Shevin, 1992). We love that analogy and see many similarities between the two. This rut-buster may be appropriate if you and your co-teaching partner are taking your relationship for granted, failing to be innovative and ignoring opportunities to grow and develop new skills. So, if you are—metaphorically speaking—spending way too many nights sitting on the couch together, donned in your sweats, grunting instead of talking, watching bad TV and eating Chinese food with plastic sporks, you may need a push forward.

A wedding and a public commitment can help to put more attention on your shared efforts, encourage gratitude and dialogue and add a festive spirit to your work together. Not quite sure how to engineer a wedding for you and your co-teaching partner? Don't worry. We thought you might "say yes" so we have already prepared a ceremony for you (see Figure 28.1)!

Sign An Agreement

Are you avowed bachelors or bachelorettes when it comes to co-teaching marriage? If so, you might try a different method for making it official. For those that prefer a more businesslike transaction, we suggest drafting an agreement or using the one we have provided (see Figure 28.2), signing on the dotted line and making your partnership legal (okay, this document won't really make your partnership legal, but it might make it feel a bit more fabulous). To make the process feel more special, consider signing with a feather pen or at least with one of those oversized souvenir pencils that can be held by both of you at once.

Form A Club

Not crazy about marriage or a formal agreement but still want to take your union up a notch? Form a co-teaching club with just you and your partner as members. Come up with a cool club name. Then vote for officers; we suggest making you and your co-teaching partner President and Vice-President. Finally, create some club rituals. Maybe you could have a sacred oath, a cool hat (think big horns and chin strap à la Fred Flintstone and the Loyal Order of the Water Buffaloes) or even a mascot (those fruit flies you are using for a science experiment will do).

TO DO LIST

- [ ] Identify that rut and climb right out of it.
- [ ] Assess your own professional life for balance. Ask your co-teaching partner for help if you feel a bit off-kilter.
- [ ] Identify something new you want to learn. Tell your co-teaching partner about it.
- [ ] Even if you are not in a big rut, try one of our "break out of your routine" ideas this week (e.g., theme day, dollar store shopping). To ensure that the break out is working, try one more.
- [ ] Consider making it official.

FIGURE 28.1

Co-Teaching Commitment Ceremony & Vows

Looking for a way to communicate your commitment to collaboration? How about getting professionally "hitched" to your co-teaching partner?

Arrange a few chairs in front of your shared desks or in front of any area of special significance to the two of you (e.g., an interactive white board, your new children-of-the-world area rug, the human skeleton model you picked out together). Fill these seats with colleagues who have supported your work so far this year; they will serve as your witnesses. Have your principal, superintendent or custodian stand before all of you to officiate. Begin the ceremony by having your officiant read the opening words.

Opening Words

We are gathered here today in the [insert location here] and in the presence of our colleagues to join together this team. If any person knows any reason these two should not be joined as co-teaching partners, speak now or forever save it for staff lounge gossip.

Then, exchange vows you have written or choose one of the options provided.

Vows: Traditional Ceremony

I _____ promise to occasionally take your lunchroom duty; do the read aloud if you need to repair the classroom laminator again; let you go to the bathroom whenever the need arises; and share responsibilities like copying, developing rubrics and making parent phone calls. Through flu season, epic IEP meetings and fire drills I promise to be your partner, unless I have a sub. I won't necessarily obey you, but I will cherish all of the times you get coffee for me. This is my solemn vow.

Vows: Contemporary Ceremony

I _____ promise to stand by you _____ through state testing, Spirit Week, parent-teacher meetings and yet another conference on rigor, readiness or relevance. If at some point, we are blessed to be able to adopt new curriculum together, I will support you in this and will stay late after school (or at least until I have to leave to get my kids/take my dog out/coach Robot Club) and plan with you to the best of my ability. I promise to honor you and respect you for at least this school year or until the administration moves one of us to a different grade level or department.

To make this ceremony as meaningful as possible, consider exchanging something as a small token of your willingness to continue growing and learning as a team (e.g., an eraser, a Bunsen burner, a pack of colorful felt tip pens, a Diet Coke).

Now that you are officially hitched, take yourselves down to the staff lounge to celebrate. You both deserve it.

FIGURE 28.2

Co-Teaching Agreement

We, the best co-teaching team in the school/district/world, agree to work together to the best of our ability for the next _____ months.

We will support each other by: _____

_____

and by _____

_____

and certainly by _____

_____ .

We will regularly incorporate these co-teaching structures into our lessons each (day/month/year):

_____

_____

_____

_____ .

We will settle disagreements by:

_____

_____ .

We will celebrate achievements by:

_____

_____ .

We hereby agree to these terms and conditions on _____ *, 20____ .*

_____ **&** _____

DAY 29

TAKE IT OUTSIDE

You are in the home stretch, friends. You and your partner have acquired new skills and competencies. You have designed new lessons. You have likely tried some new teaching strategies. And you have probably explored and expanded your roles in the last few weeks. After all of that, you may feel ready to hit the classroom floor running or… you may be feeling some panic. After all, this is the second-to-last section of our book, and you are probably beginning to realize that we don't have a lot more to share.

Are these thinning pages causing you a little anxiety? Still have questions?

Don't worry. We anticipated that thirty days of information would not be enough for some learning-loving co-teaching teams, so we wanted to share some of our favorite outside resources for continued exploration of this topic. On Day 29 we are providing you with a list of co-teaching-themed films, books, articles and websites. We have used these resources in our own work and hope you will find them as helpful as we have. Reference this list for lesson planning, developing in-house staff development activities or stocking a co-teaching library.

Films/Movie Clips

» Friend, Marilyn. *The Power of Two: Making a Difference Through Co-Teaching*, (2nd ed.). Port Chester, NY: National Professional Resources, 2005.

» Friend, Marilyn, L. Burrello, and J. Burrello. *More Power! Instruction in Co-Taught Classrooms.* Bloomington, IN: The Forum on Education, 2009.

» Kluth, Paula. *You're Going to Love This Kid! A Professional Development Package for Teaching Students with Autism in the Inclusive Classroom.* Baltimore: Paul H. Brookes/Landlocked Films, 2011.

» The Teaching Channel: www.teaching-channel.org

Books

» Beninghof, Anne M. *Co-Teaching That Works.* San Francisco, CA: Jossey-Bass, 2011.

» Chapman, Carrie and Cate Hart Hyatt. *Critical Conversations in Co-Teaching.* Bloomington, IN: Solution Tree, 2011.

» Conderman, Greg, Val Bresnahan, and Theresa Petersen. *Purposeful Co-Teaching: Real Cases and Effective Strategies.* Thousand Oaks, CA: Corwin, 2009.

» Dieker, Lisa A. *The Co-Teaching Lesson Plan Book.* Whitefish Bay, WI: Knowledge by Design, 2006.

» Friend, Marilyn. *Co-Teach! A Manual for Creating and Sustaining Classroom Partnerships in Inclusive Schools* (2nd ed.). Greensboro, NC: Marilyn Friend, Inc., 2014.

» Friend, Marilyn, and Lynne Cook. *Interactions: Collaboration Skills for School Professionals* (6th ed.). Columbus, OH: Merrill, 2010.

» Murawski, Wendy W. *Collaborative Teaching in Elementary Schools: Making the Co-Teaching Marriage Work!* Thousand Oaks, CA : Corwin Press, 2010.

» Murawski, Wendy W. *Collaborative Teaching in Secondary Schools: Making the Co-Teaching Marriage Work!* Thousand Oaks, CA: Corwin Press, 2009.

» Villa, Richard A., Jacqueline S. Thousand, and Ann Nevin. *A Guide to Co-Teaching: Practical Tips for Facilitating Student Learning* (3rd ed.). Thousand Oaks, CA: Corwin Press, 2013.

Articles

» Beninghof, Anne. "To Clone or Not to Clone?" *Educational Leadership* 73(4), (2016): 10-15.

» Bouck, Emily C. "Co-Teaching… Not Just a Textbook Term: Implications for Practice." *Preventing School Failure* 51(2), (2007): 46–51.

» Dieker, Lisa A. "What Are the Characteristics of 'Effective' Middle and High School Co-Taught Teams for Students With Disabilities?" *Preventing School Failure: Alternative Education for Children and Youth* 46(1), (2001): 14–23.

» Dieker, Lisa A., and Wendy W. Murawski. "Co-Teaching at the Secondary Level: Unique Issues, Current Tends, and Suggestions for Success." *The High School Journal* 86(4), (2003): 1–13.

» Friend, Marilyn. "The Co-Teaching Partnership." *Educational Leadership* 64(5) (2007): 58–62

» Friend, Marilyn, Lynne Cook, DeAnna Hurley-Chamberlain, and Cynthia Shamberger. "Co-Teaching: An Illustration of the Complexity of Collaboration in Special Education." *Journal of Educational and Psychological Consultation* 20(1) (2010): 9–27.

» Giangreco, Michael F., Jesse C. Suter, and Sean M. Hurley. "Revisiting Personnel Utilization in Inclusion-Oriented Schools." *Journal of Special Education* 47(2) (2013): 121–132.

» Kluth, Paula, and Diana Straut. "Do as We Say and as We Do: Teaching and Modeling Collaborative Practice in the University Classroom." *Journal of Teacher Education* 54(3) (2003): 228–240.

» Knachendoffel, E. Ann. "Collaborative Teaming in the Secondary School." *Exceptional Children* 40(4) (2007): 1–20.

» Kohler-Evans, Patty A. "Co-Teaching: How to Make This Marriage Work in Front of the Kids." *Education* 127(2) (2006): 260–264.

» Magiera, Kathleen, Cynthia Smith, Naomi Zigmond, and Kelli Gebauer. "Benefits of Co-Teaching in Secondary Mathematics Classes." *Teaching Exceptional Children* 37(3) (2005): 20–24.

» Mandel, Kenneth, and Terry Eiserman. "Team Teaching in High School." *Educational Leadership* 73(4), (2016): 74-77.

» Mastropieri, Margo A., Thomas E. Scruggs, Janet Graetz, Jennifer Norland, Walena Gardizi, and Kimberly McDuffie. "Case Studies in Co-Teaching in the Content Areas: Successes, Failures, and Challenges." *Intervention in School and Clinic* 40(5) (2005): 260–270.

» Murawski, Wendy, and Lisa Dieker. "50 Ways to Keep Your Co-Teacher: Strategies for Before, During, and After Co-Teaching." *Teaching Exceptional Children* 40(4) (2008): 40–48.

» Murawski, Wendy, and Wendy Lochner. "Observing Co-Teaching: What to Ask for, Look for, and Listen for." *Intervention in School and Clinic* 46(3) (2010): 174–183.

» Murdock, Linda, and David Finneran, Kristin Theve. "Co-Teaching to Reach Every Learner." *Educational Leadership* 73(4), (2016): 42-47.

» Rea, P. J., and J. Connell. "A Guide to Co-Teaching." *Developing Exemplary Teachers* (2005): 36–41.

» Scruggs, Thomas. E., Margo A. Mastropieri, and Kimberly A. McDuffie. "Co-Teaching in Inclusive Classrooms: A Metasynthesis of Qualitative Research." *Exceptional Children* 73(4) (2007): 392–416.

» Sileo, Jane M. "Co-Teaching: Getting to Know your Partner." *Teaching Exceptional Children* 43(5) (2011): 32-38.

» Sileo, Jane M., and D. VanGarderen. "Creating Optimal Opportunities to Learn Mathematics: Blending Co-Teaching Structures with Research-Based Practices." *Teaching Exceptional Children* 42(3) (2010): 14-21.

» Wilson, Gloria Lodato. "This Doesn't Look Familiar: A Supervisor's Guide for Observing Co-Teachers." *Intervention in School and Clinic* 40(5) (2005): 271–275.

» Wilson, Gloria Lodato. "Be an Active Co-Teacher." *Intervention in School and Clinic* 43(4) (2008): 240–243.

Websites

» 2 Teach
www.2teachllc.com

» CEC Reality 101: Collaboration
www.cecreality101.org/category/
collaboration-and-co-teaching

» Collaboration & Co-Teaching:
Strategies for English Learners
coteachingforells.weebly.com

» The Co-Taught Classroom
www.cotaughtclassroom.com

» The Co-Teaching Connection
www.marilynfriend.com

» Differentiation Daily
www.differentiationdaily.com

» Ideas For Educators
www.ideasforeducators.com

» Dr. Julie Causton
www.inclusiveschooling.com

» Middle Web: Two Teachers in the Room
www.middleweb.com/category/
two-teachers-in-the-room

» Dr. Paula Kluth
www.paulakluth.com

» Dr. Patrick Schwarz
www.patrickschwarz.com

» Dr. Richard Villa
www.ravillabayridge.com

» Vanderbilt's Effective School Practices:
Promoting Collaboration & Monitoring
Students' Academic Achievement
iris.peabody.vanderbilt.edu/module/esp

TO DO LIST

- [ ] Select and explore one item from each category in this section.
- [ ] Pass these resources on to other teams in your building.
- [ ] Consider creating a co-teaching professional library. Don't forget to add multiple copies of this book.

DAY 30

CELEBRATE

That's it. You made it to the last day of the month, and if we know you, your team is firing on all cylinders, meeting collaborative goals and making it all look easy. If this is true (and even if only parts of it are true), you deserve a bit of a celebration.

Co-teaching teams sometimes get down to the business of planning, teaching and evaluating to such a degree that they forget to admire their accomplishments. The most effective teams, however, find ways to be reflective, pat themselves on the back and enjoy one another's company. Co-teaching can be tough, especially when you are a novice co-teacher or when you are taking on new roles and different responsibilities. For this reason alone, you and your partner need an occasional celebration. This practice can help both of you stay positive and productive.

Day 30 is filled with different ways to celebrate with your team and your students. We have you covered from reasons to cheer, to party supplies, to celebration rituals. So, top off your Hawaiian Punch, strap on your party hats (careful not to let the elastic bands snap your chins) and read on.

Celebration Inspiration

Celebrate your accomplishments, however large or small. Celebrate progress on your individual or team goals. Celebrate getting through a few tough weeks. Celebrate that you are remembering to celebrate.

We are hoping that you and your co-teaching partner can think of many reasons to pop open the Pringles and crank up the old boom box, but if you need help, see Table 30.1 for ideas galore.

TABLE 30.1

Causes for Celebration in the Co-Taught Classroom

Not sure what to celebrate? Pat yourselves on the back for:

» teaching a phenomenal lesson

» achieving a breakthrough with one or more students

» building satisfying relationships with families

» running an efficient meeting

» making impressive progress toward a co-teaching goal

» role-sharing or role-swapping in a new way

» busting out of a lesson-planning or classroom-instruction rut

» developing a great new parity signal

» communicating, problem solving or planning better than ever before

» getting to school every day this week

» trying a new co-teaching structure

» trying a new differentiation technique

» finishing this book/trying ideas from this book/ successfully using this book as a door stop, prop in a hilarious classroom skit or heavy-duty fly swatter

---

Supplies

Once you have the cause for your celebration, it will be time to gather supplies. You never know when the mood will strike to throw a little party for you and your co-teaching partner, for your entire team or for your whole class, so don't wait for a special occasion to shop for confetti. Keep a box stocked with celebration supplies and be on the lookout for occasions to unpack the contents.

Talk to one another about what sorts of items would make up the perfect celebration kit. If you both love sweets, you might need a stash of chocolate. If you are music lovers, your kit might contain some portable speakers, microphones and maybe even a strobe light. See Table 30. 2 for a list of other celebration supplies you may want to keep on hand.

TABLE 30.2
Celebration Supplies for the Co-Taught Classroom

You can have a celebration without party supplies, but you can have an even better celebration with a few props and decorations. Browse this list to determine what you want to keep in your celebration kit:

» note cards to write memos to anyone you want to celebrate (e.g., each other, families, students, the recess supervisor, the wise administrator who engineered your co-teaching partnership)

» party hats

» feather boas

» colorful markers for creating your notes, signs, banners and posters

» party playlists

» karaoke machine

» confetti

» glitter

» streamers

» disco ball

» party games

» life-size cardboard cutouts of you and your co-teaching partner decked out in formal wear

---

Types Of Celebrations

There are as many types of celebrations as there are candies in that frog-shaped piñata you have been eyeing at the party store (and yes, attacking it and enjoying the spoils with your co-teaching partner would be a great way to celebrate a day of dissections in Biology). Don't feel like your co-teaching team has to mimic the what, where and when of other teams' celebrations. Your celebrations should be as unique as your co-teaching team itself. For starters, consider some of our favorite rituals, toasts and hold-the-confetti happenings.

Traditions & Rituals

Traditions and rituals are as important in schools as they are in families. Regular celebration inspires both connection and reflection. And since successful teaming isn't always something that schools get recognized for, it is critical that educators themselves take time to acknowledge how very powerful and important their daily work, commitment and decisions are to the lives of the learners in their care. Here are some traditions co-teaching teams we know have used:

» *Once a year, a team goes to a professional baseball game in their city. Leading up to the game, the team identifies everything they are celebrating. They have cheered everything from students going to college, to a mini-grant being funded, to being invited to present at a regional inclusion conference.*

» *One group of co-teachers has a lunch during the last week of the school year to celebrate successes. Each team shares accomplishments during the meal.*

» *A co-teaching team regularly surprises colleagues and one another with recycled gifts to celebrate achievements. For instance, one teacher gave the other salt-and-pepper shakers as a celebration of their new differentiation techniques. The note read, "Thank you for helping me 'shake up' the lessons in our classroom." And when the school psychologist helped the team understand a student better, they awarded him a huge pair of tinted spectacles and extended gratitude for his role in helping them see the learner "with rose-colored glasses."*

» *Another team has an Oscar–style presentation at the end of the year. They use school supplies (e.g., string, glitter, glue) to create their awards and present them to one another at a small ceremony in the library.*

» *A teaching team consisting of two middle school teachers and a paraprofessional has a "highlight reel" celebration on the first day of each month. They enjoy breakfast together in their classroom and each one of them talks for a few minutes about what they see as the high points or good news of the previous month. This process serves as a way for these educators to pat one another on the back as they commonly talk about their own successes and about the successes they see their teammates having.*

» *Two co-teaching teams celebrate something every Friday afternoon. They go out after school for exactly one hour and have a little something to eat and drink. After some small talk, each person shares one celebration of the week (e.g., "Bryson can transition through the building without any adult support now").*

Toasts

Grab your soda, fruit-and-carbonated fancy water or sparkling apple juice and propose a toast. Raise glasses at the end of each week, at the end of hard meetings or just as the mood strikes. Be sure to take turns being the designated toastmaster. See Table 30.3 for a list of toasts you may want to use with your co-teaching partner.

TABLE 30.3

Co-Teaching Toasts

Use these toasts the next time you have reason to celebrate in your shared classroom:

To us...for making it to the end of our water cycle unit without drowning

To us...for figuring out twenty-seven ways to teach algebra vocabulary

To us...for fixing the computer cart without calling for help

To us...for creating peer mentoring relationships that are as close to perfect as perfect can be

To us...for our stunning five-minute reenactment of an entire chapter of *The Lightning Thief*

To us...for banging out parent-teacher conferences with so many glowing reviews from our families

To us...for teaching the best World War II unit ever and for rocking our Rosie the Riveter costumes

To us...for meeting our goal of personally touching base with every single student in our co-taught classroom today

To us...for positively problem solving yesterday

To us...for making it all the way to Wednesday afternoon

To us...for running one of the most productive eight-minute team meetings ever

To us...for using station teaching three days in a row and mastering the timing of the rotations

To us...for staying healthy during flu season

To us...for adding thirty new titles to our classroom library without breaking the bank

To us...for catching Abrahamster Lincoln, the class pet, pretty much without incident

To us...for helping our students achieve the best scores we have ever seen on the Chapter 9 chemistry quiz

To us...for singing a great duet (about infant CPR) while we were duet teaching

Hold-The-Confetti Happenings

If balloons, streamers and big outings do not do it for you, you can still have a celebration. Some co-teaching teams like to bond in a quieter way. Calmer co-teaching duos may want to celebrate by perusing the newest edition of the *Oriental Trading* catalog or sitting side-by-side to watch adorable cat videos on YouTube.

Need more ideas? See Table 30.4 for activities that help teams celebrate in an everyday sort of way.

TABLE 30.4

Hold-the-Confetti Happenings

Not all celebrations need to be loud, long or outrageous. These simple activities can remind you and your partner to pause for a collaborative pat on the back. Celebrate by:

» ordering lunch in

» starting or ending the day with a few fist pumps

» enjoying a great co-created Pandora channel as you collaboratively prepare materials

» engaging in a series of elaborate high-fives and handshakes

» giving a thumbs-up from across the room

» writing five reasons your partner totally rocks (on a rock)

» taking fun, commemorative selfies

» going to a school event together (e.g., play, basketball game)

» sharing a bag of pretzels from the vending machine and breaking the last one in half so you can each have a piece

» putting sticky notes on each other's desks to say "thank you", "good job" or "I love splitting bags of pretzels with you"

Don't Forget The Students

Hey, hey, hey…you, yes, you in the clown wig, tulle tutu and "party hardy" removable tattoo on your forehead, we are thrilled that you are celebrating your team's good news. In all of your excitement, however, try not to forget your students. Every single celebration need not involve them, but some of them absolutely should. Take a moment to consider how you might include learners in honoring good news. Need inspiration? Browse Table 30.5 and grab some of our suggestions.

TABLE 30.5
Student Celebrations for the Co-Taught Classroom

When you involve students in your celebrations, it doesn't have to take a lot of class time or planning time. These ideas can work just as well in high school as they can in the early grades and none of them require much in the way of money, forethought or space. Involve students in celebrations with:

» one-song dance parties

» flash-mob practices/performances

» dress-up days (e.g., pajamas, school colors, curricular theme)

» a juice or hot cider toast

» a short popcorn break

» an inspirational movie or interesting content-themed feature film

» a reading day where students get to spend an extended amount of time with texts they choose

» an innovation day where students get to spend an extended amount of time with a project they choose

» five-minute appreciations where students take turns recognizing others who have helped them or done something notable

» an exhibition of student art, writing, films or skits

» a game of content-related trivia, charades or hangman

» the creation of a content-related piece of collaborative art

» a ten-minute "good news hunt" where students rush to capture positive news, pictures and video with cameras, iPads or computers

» a classroom talent show

» a group-selected guest speaker

Keep It Going

We think co-teaching can provide some of the best opportunities for interesting, creative and powerful pedagogy. So "cheers" to a great school year. We are both wearing party hats, blowing noisemakers and tossing confetti over your heads (figuratively speaking, anyway). We are encouraging you and supporting you and celebrating your accomplishments and all of the very powerful co-teaching moments that you have already experienced and that await you in the months to come. Congratulations on your union, your growth and your journey and on all of the successes that have occurred thus far in the classroom due to your collaborative efforts. Keep up the great work, team!

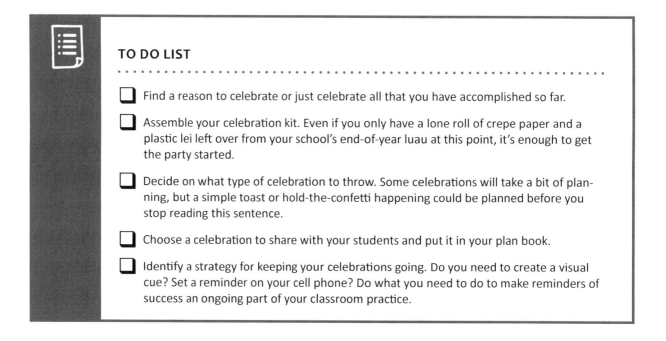

TO DO LIST

- ☐ Find a reason to celebrate or just celebrate all that you have accomplished so far.

- ☐ Assemble your celebration kit. Even if you only have a lone roll of crepe paper and a plastic lei left over from your school's end-of-year luau at this point, it's enough to get the party started.

- ☐ Decide on what type of celebration to throw. Some celebrations will take a bit of planning, but a simple toast or hold-the-confetti happening could be planned before you stop reading this sentence.

- ☐ Choose a celebration to share with your students and put it in your plan book.

- ☐ Identify a strategy for keeping your celebrations going. Do you need to create a visual cue? Set a reminder on your cell phone? Do what you need to do to make reminders of success an ongoing part of your classroom practice.

REFERENCES

Andrade, Jackie. "What Does Doodling Do?" *Applied Cognitive Psychology* 24(1) (2010): 100–106.

Aronson, Elliot, and Shelley Patnoe. *The Jigsaw Classroom: Building Cooperation in the Classroom* (2nd ed.). New York: Addison Wesley Longman, 1997.

Carlson, Richard. *Don't Sweat the Small Stuff and It's All Small Stuff: Simple Ways to Keep the Little Things from Taking over Your Life.* New York, NY: Hyperion, 1997.

Causton, Julie, and George Theoharis. *The Principal's Handbook for Leading Inclusive Schools.* Baltimore, MD: Paul H. Brookes, 2014.

Chen, Greg. "School Disorder and Student Achievement." *Journal of School Violence* 6(1) (2007): 27–43.

Cook, Lynne, and Marilyn Friend. "Co-Teaching: Guidelines for Creating Effective Practices." *Focus on Exceptional Children* 28(3) (1995): 1–16.

Dodge, Bernie. "WebQuests: A Technique for Internet-based Learning." *Distance Educator* 1 (2) (1995): 10–13.

Draper, Roni Jo. "Active Learning in Mathematics: Desktop Teaching." *Mathematics Teacher* 90 (8) (1997): 622–25.

Ford, Allison. "Wisconsin School Inclusion Project: A Team Planning Packet For Inclusive Education." (1995).

Freeman, Scott, Sarah L. Eddy, Miles McDonough, Michelle K. Smith, Nnadozie Okoroafor, Hannah Jordt, and Mary Pat Wenderoth. "Active Learning Increases Student Performance In Science, Engineering, And Mathematics." *Proceedings of the National Academy of Sciences,* 111 (23) (2014): 8410–8415.

Gardner, Howard. *Frames of Mind: The Theory of Multiple Intelligences.* New York: Basic Books, 1983.

Garmston, Robert J., and Bruce M. Wellman. *The Adaptive School: A Sourcebook for Developing Collaborative Groups.* Norwood, MA: Christopher Gordon, 1999.

Gent, Pamela J. *Great Ideas: Using Service-Learning and Differentiated Instruction to Help Your Students Succeed.* Baltimore, MD: Paul H. Brookes, 2009.

Giangreco, Michael F. *Absurdities and Realities of Special Education: The Complete Digital Set* [searchable CD]. Thousand Oaks, CA: Corwin, 2007.

Giangreco, Michael F., Susan W. Edelman, and Stephen M. Broer. "Respect, Appreciation, and Acknowledgment of Paraprofessionals Who Support Students With Disabilities." *Exceptional Children* 67(4) 2001: 485–498.

Giangreco, Michael F., Jesse C. Suter, and Victoria Graf. "Roles of Team Members Supporting Students With Disabilities in Inclusive Classrooms." In *Choosing Outcomes and Accommodations for Children: A Guide to Educational Planning for Students With Disabilities,* 3rd ed., 197-204. Edited by Michael F. Giangreco, Chigee J. Cloninger and Virginia Salce Iverson. Baltimore: Paul H. Brookes, 2011.

Grandin, Temple. Thinking in Pictures. London, UK: Bloomsbury Publishing, 1995.

Greene, Marci S., and Madelyn L. Isaacs. "The Responsibility of Modeling Collaboration in the University Education Classroom." *Action in Teacher Education* 20 (1999): 98–106.

Hertz-Lazarowitz, Rachel, Spencer Kagan, Shlomo Sharan, Robert Slavin, and Clark Webb (Eds.). *Learning to Cooperate, Cooperating to Learn.* New York, NY: Springer Science+Business Media, LLC, 2013.

Holt, John. *How Children Learn.* New York, NY: Pitman, 1967.

Howard, Lori, and Elizabeth A. Potts. "Using Co-Planning Time: Strategies for a Successful Co-Teaching Marriage." *TEACHING Exceptional Children Plus* 5(4) (2009).

Kagan, Spencer. "The Structural Approach to Cooperative Learning." *Educational Leadership* 47(4) (1989): 12-15.

Kluth, Paula. "Community-Referenced Learning and the Inclusive Classroom." *Remedial and Special Education* 21(1) (2000): 19–26.

Kluth, Paula, and Kelly Chandler-Olcott. "Why Everyone Benefits from Including Students With Autism in Literacy Classrooms." *The Reading Teacher* 62(7) (2009): 548–557.

Kluth, Paula, and Sheila Danaher. *From Tutor Scripts to Talking Sticks: 100 Ways to Differentiate Instruction in K–12 Inclusive Classrooms.* Baltimore, MD: Paul H. Brookes, 2013.

Kluth, Paula, and Diana Straut. "Do as We Say and as We Do: Teaching and Modeling Collaborative Practice in the University Classroom." *Journal of Teacher Education,* 54 (3) (2003): 228–240.

Kohler-Evans, Patty A. *Co-Teaching: How to Make this Marriage Work in Front of the Kids.* Education, 127, 260–264, 2006.

Ladson-Billings, Gloria. *The Dreamkeepers: Successful Teachers of African-American Students.* San Francisco, CA: Jossey-Bass, 1994.

Lamke, Susan, Denise Pratt, and Stan Graeve. *Safe and Healthy Secondary Schools.* Boys Town, NE: Boys Town Press, 2009.

Mazur, Eric. "Farewell, Lecture?" *Science* 323 (2009): 50–51.

Morris, Robert (Ed.). *Solving the Problems of Youth At-Risk: Involving Parents and Community Resources.* Lancaster, PA: Technomic, 1992.

Murawski, Wendy. *Collaborative Teaching in Secondary Schools: Making the Co-Teaching Marriage Work!* Thousand Oaks, CA: Corwin Press, 2009.

O'Donnell-Allen, Cindy. *The Book Club Companion: Fostering Strategic Readers in the Secondary Classroom.* Portsmouth, NH: Heinemann, 2006.

Parker, J. F. *Workshops for Active Learning.* Delta, BC: JFP Productions, 1990.

Reis, Sally M., and Joseph S. Renzulli. "Using Curriculum Compacting to Challenge the Above-Average." *Educational Leadership* 50 (2) (1992): 51–57.

Ripski, Michael B., and Anne Gregory. "Unfair, Unsafe, and Unwelcome: Do High School Students' Perceptions of Unfairness, Hostility, and Victimization in School Predict Engagement and Achievement?" *Journal of School Violence* 8(4) (2009): 355–375.

Roosa, J. B. "SOCS: Situations, Options, Consequences, Simulations: A Technique for Teaching Social Interactions." Paper presented at the American Psychological Association, Montreal, Canada, 1973.

Sapon-Shevin, Mara. Introduction: "Marriage Advice." In J. Thousand and R. Villa (Eds.), *Restructuring for Caring and Effective Education: An Administrative Guide to Creating Heterogeneous Schools* pp. 3–6. Baltimore, MD: Paul H. Brookes, 1992.

Schwarz, Patrick, and Paula Kluth. *You're Welcome: 30 Innovative Ideas for the Inclusive Classroom.* Portsmouth, NH: Heinemann, 2007.

Scruggs, Thomas E., Margo A. Mastropieri, and Kimberly A. McDuffie. "Co-Teaching in Inclusive Classrooms: A Metasynthesis of Qualitative Research." *Exceptional Children* 73 (4) (2007): 392–416.

Senge, Peter. *The Fifth Discipline: The Art and Practice of the Learning Organization.* New York, NY: Currency/Doubleday, 2006.

Shapiro-Barnard, Susan. Preparing the Ground for What Is to Come: A Rationale for Inclusive High Schools. In *Restructuring High Schools for All Students—Taking Inclusion to the Next Level,* 1–14. Edited by Cheryl Jorgensen. Baltimore, MD: Paul H. Brookes, 1998.

Sharan, Y., and S. Sharan. "Group Investigation in the Cooperative Classroom." *Handbook of Cooperative Learning Methods* (1994): 97–114.

Tamm, James W., and Ronald J. Luyet. *Radical Collaboration: Five Essential Skills to Overcome Defensiveness and Build Successful Relationships.* New York, NY: Harper Business, 2004.

Udvari-Solner, Alice, and Paula Kluth, (Eds.). *Joyful Learning: Active and Collaborative Learning in Inclusive Classrooms.* Thousand Oaks, CA: Corwin Press, 2008.

Udvari-Solner, Alice. "Examining Teacher Thinking: Constructing a Process to Design Curricular Adaptations." *Remedial and Special Education* 17 (4) (1996): 245–254.

Yoder, Denise I., E. Retish, and R. Wade. "Service Learning: Meeting Student and Community Needs." *Teaching Exceptional Children* 28(4), (1996): 14–18.

LITERARY REFERENCES

Halberstein, David. *The Children*. New York: Fawcett Books, 2000.

Lee, Harper. *To Kill a Mockingbird*. New York: Warner, 1982.

Levinson, Cynthia. *We've Got a Job: The 1963 Birmingham Children's March*. Atlanta, GA: Peachtree Publishers, Ltd. 2012.

Rawlinson, Julia. *Fletcher and the Falling Leaves*. New York: HarperCollins, 2008.

Riordan, Rick. *The Lightning Thief*. New York: Hyperion Books, 2005.

Skloot, Rebecca. *The Immortal Life of Henrietta Lacks*. New York: Crown Publishers, 2010.

White, E. B. *Charlotte's Web*. New York: Harper & Brothers, 1952.

Zusak, Markus. *The Book Thief*. New York: Knopf Books, 2005.

ABOUT THE AUTHORS

Dr. Paula Kluth is an author, educational consultant and advocate. Her work is centered on providing inclusive opportunities for students with disabilities and creating more responsive and engaging schooling experiences for all. She is a former special educator who has served as a classroom teacher and inclusion facilitator. Her professional interests include differentiating instruction, inclusive schooling and collaboration.

Paula is the author or co-author of twelve books including *From Text Maps to Memory Caps: 100 Ways to Differentiate Instruction in K-12 Inclusive Classrooms; Don't We Already Do Inclusion?: 100 Ways to Improve Inclusive Schools; You're Going to Love This Kid: Teaching Students with Autism in Inclusive Classrooms; Joyful Learning: Active and Collaborative Learning in the Inclusive Classroom and The Autism Checklist.*

Paula loves the Green Bay Packers, is afraid of snakes and small aircraft (and snakes on small aircraft) and wishes everyone would include, differentiate, collaborate and randomly offer her small gifts of Sharpies and chocolates. You can learn more about Paula and her work by visiting her professional website: www.paulakluth.com, by following her on Twitter (@PaulaKluth) and Pinterest (www.pinterest.com/paulapin/) or by joining her on Facebook at www.facebook.com/paulakluth.

Dr. Julie Causton is a professor at Syracuse University, author and independent consultant. Her work is deeply guided by her passion for inclusive engaging education for ALL students. A former elementary, middle and high school teacher, she knows firsthand the joys and challenges of co-teaching. Her professional interests include best practices in inclusive schooling, inclusive school reform, differentiation, humanistic behavioral supports and collaboration. She has authored six books on these topics designed for paraprofessionals, administrators, educators and related service providers. She has authored over thirty articles in journals such as *Exceptional Children, Teaching Exceptional Children, Journal of Research in Childhood Education, International Journal of Inclusive Education, Behavioral Disorders, Studies in Art Education, Camping Magazine, Remedial and Special Education* and *Equity and Excellence in Education.* Julie loves time management books, cardstock, to-do lists, rubrics and colorful fifteen-minute-increment schedules. She fears bats, loves hummingbirds and secretly hopes Oprah will have her as a guest on Super Soul Sunday. She dreams of a day when the question of school inclusion for every student is answered with a resounding, "Of course!" You can learn more about Julie and her work by visiting www.inclusiveschooling.com, by following her on Twitter (@JulieCauston) or by joining her on Facebook at www.facebook.com/InspireInclusion.

Both authors live for inclusive education, love writing and teaching about supporting diverse learners, have given hundreds of presentations to educators, are University of Wisconsin-Madison graduates and never say "no" to a pumpkin spice latte. This duo has been called the "Tina Fey and Amy Poehler of co-teaching" (okay, maybe it was only once...by their moms...but still). You can learn more about their shared work by visiting www.cotaughtclassroom.com or by joining them on their Facebook page at www.facebook.com/cotaughtclassroom.

THANK YOU & A FAVOR

Thank you so much for reading *30 Days to the Co-Taught Classroom*. We sincerely hope the book has provided you with opportunities to acquire new skills and competencies and has helped you create the best possible collaborative relationship with your co-teaching partner.

If it has been useful, we would be soooo very grateful if you could do us a small favor. We would simply like you to recommend this book to anyone you think might like it, including anyone who co-teaches, anyone who has heard of co-teaching and anyone who could use "co-teaching" in a sentence. If you really like this book, we would love it if you would recommend it on Amazon.com, Goodreads.com and related sites. If you don't like this book, please don't tell a soul.

Again, thank you so much for reading. Now go out there and co-teach your hearts out. You got this!